The Lost Season

Also By Stacey May Fowles

NON-FICTION

Baseball Life Advice (2017)

FICTION

Infidelity (2013)

Fear of Fighting (2008)

Be Good (2007)

FOR CHILDREN

The Invitation (2023)

ANTHOLOGIES

Good Mom on Paper: Writers on Creativity and Motherhood (co-edited with Jen Sookfong Lee, 2022)

Whatever Gets You Through: Twelve Survivors on Life after Sexual Assault (co-edited with Jen Sookfong Lee, 2019)

Best Canadian Sportswriting (co-edited with Pasha Malla, 2017)

She's Shameless: Women write about growing up, rocking out and fighting back (co-edited with Megan Griffith-Greene, 2009)

The Lost Season

A Memoir of Infertility, Motherhood, and the Worry and Work Demanded of Women

Stacey May Fowles

McCLELLAND & STEWART

Hardcover edition published 2026

Library and Archives Canada Cataloguing in Publication
Title: The lost season : a memoir of infertility, motherhood, and the worry and work demanded of women / Stacey May Fowles.
Names: Fowles, Stacey May, author
Identifiers: Canadiana (print) 20260020311 | Canadiana (ebook) 2026002032X | ISBN 9780771030116 (hardcover) | ISBN 9780771030123 (EPUB)
Subjects: LCSH: Fowles, Stacey May. | LCSH: Motherhood—Psychological aspects. | LCSH: Motherhood—Social aspects. | LCSH: Infertility—Psychological aspects. | LCGFT: Essays. Classification: LCC HQ759 .F69 2026 | DDC 306.874/3—dc23

Cover design by Andrew Roberts
Cover art: Tetiana Gorbatyuk / Getty
Typeset in Mercury Text G1 by Erin Cooper and Six Red Marbles
Printed in Canada

McClelland & Stewart
A division of Penguin Random House Canada
320 Front Street West, Suite 1400
Toronto, Ontario, M5V 3B6, Canada
penguinrandomhouse.ca

1 2 3 4 5 30 29 28 27 26

New motherhood is a lost season.

It both defines and leaves you adrift.

The sky is golden but it burns.

Contents

INTRODUCTION

On Not Writing About Motherhood

It's the end of my first summer of being a mother, and a male writer friend, an English professor who has published an award-winning, bestselling non-fiction book that book clubs absolutely love, sends me an email.

"Any chance you'd like to escape for an afternoon and come talk to my young non-fictioneers this fall?"

The impromptu invite feels like a kind of rescue—a rope hurled across the wide crevasse separating my exciting old life as a freelance writer from my new, rather repetitive and all-consuming one as a mother. I'm in month six of staying at home with my new baby and, well, "struggling." My once busy inbox hasn't been serving up a lot of paid assignments, so this unsolicited offer to come back to the working world, however briefly, is certainly welcome. Beyond that, the idea of actually talking to adults about something other than the minutia of breast and bottle feedings and sleeping through the night is tantalizing.

I rejoice and immediately say yes.

I'd done this visit to my friend's class to talk to his students about being a "professional writer" in years past and loved it. It always seems to be scheduled at the very moment in the year when I become disillusioned with the business of putting words on a page. I'm of course grateful to get paid to write in any capacity, but a sort of existential "what is it all for" tends to settle in at least once annually—this churning out thousands and thousands of words on all sorts of subjects, for newspapers and magazines and sports websites, this scrambling to shake enough hands, sign enough contracts, and send out enough tiny invoices to make literary ends meet.

And then, like well-timed magic, I get to spend a few afternoon hours with a group of brilliant, enthusiastic writers who are not yet twenty years old. Writers who are hopeful, and thoughtful, and just love the written word. Writers who don't care about the details of deals, or awards, or which book agent is best. Bylines, and galas, and literary insider status don't even cross their minds. Instead, they want nothing more than to simply be writers—or even better, to simply write—and every year I walk out of my friend's small nonfiction class re-energized and full of gratitude.

But this particular year I feel more imposter than professional writer. I've only written about three thousand words in the eight months prior to this invitation—which feels pretty dismal given the fact that I'd probably written over a hundred thousand in any given year before. I invoiced for a whole two pieces in the half year after my daughter was born, when previously it was not uncommon for me to pay the bills by publishing at least a piece a week. Being a freelancer on "maternity leave" means I'm barely paying any bills at all, relying heavily on my husband's income to keep things going in our household—a privileged but also deeply humbling experience.

Beyond that, all the bookish invites to launches and parties and ceremonies—the things that seem to prove you're actually a writer worth caring about—have evaporated. My professional social life has disappeared, like I've been sent to the new-mom corner of literature. I play out imaginary conversations in my mind:

"What happened to her?"

"Oh, she had a *baby*."

I am—embarrassingly—bitter about this, while also disgruntled, looking for someone to blame. Mostly though, I'm demoralized and suffering a pretty clichéd identity crisis. I certainly don't think I have any wisdom to impart to young minds.

My kindly English professor/bestselling award-winning author friend immediately and generously dismisses all these worries. As a beleaguered father himself, he assures me I have lots to offer his young scribes. He thinks my coming in while on the freelancer's version of maternity leave (read: no income) will actually be a good dose of reality for them, giving them a more complete picture of the potential struggles and ups and downs of the job and how life so often complicates the intoxicating dreamy romanticism of "being a writer."

In our subsequent email exchange, he asks after my daughter and I let him know she's "a pretty chill baby." Thankfully, she's just entered the phase where she can sit up and entertain herself for a bit, smearing recently introduced solids on the plastic tray of her high chair or grabbing at the rainbow-coloured plastic toys on her Fisher-Price activity centre.

"It's amazing what a difference it makes to be able to just make a cup of tea or a phone call," I write.

He then encourages me to bring her along—an offer I am grateful for given how often it seems I want to go to spaces where she is either explicitly or implicitly unwelcome—but I feel comfortable confessing to him that I'm actually looking forward to the time on my own.

At this point in her life, I hardly ever get any time alone.

On the bus on the way to the university, while I am psyching myself up to be professional, organized, and instructive, I notice there is a baby-related stain on my shirt.

I can't discern whether it is breast milk or vomited-up breast milk.

Instead of reviewing my notes for the afternoon's session, I nod off during the forty-minute ride. Between pregnancy and postpartum, I haven't slept more than three or four hours at a stretch in over a year. In desperation my husband and I have started throwing money at a consultant to solve what we're calling "the sleep problem." This cost has not yet translated into success, and most of the time I walk around in a barely coherent fog, which isn't ideal for university instruction. I am not only intensely sleep deprived but also unbelievably lonely, spending most of my limited energy on labour-intensive (and entirely frustrating) sleep training and almost all my time with a tiny person who is unable to communicate beyond screaming and crying. I rarely find myself in casual conversation beyond the topic of diapers, solids, or milestones.

Because of all this, being back at the university to talk to students is both thrilling and intimidating. As I hop off the bus and hunt for the imposing brutalist-style humanities building, I feel like a fascinated alien visiting from another planet. I'm early, and the aforementioned sleepy fog means I get lost in a maze of concrete corridors on my way to my friend's office. I revel in the luxury of getting lost on my own.

When I do finally find him, I am deeply thrilled to talk to a grown-up who is not my husband, or the librarian who leads the local story time, or my baby's doctor. With about an hour until class begins, we sit across from each other in his tiny, fluorescent-lit academic office, surrounded by his very serious adult books and very serious adult paperwork. We drink coffee from paper cups the way adults who enjoy each other's company do. (Mine, of course, is decaf because god forbid I keep my daughter up with my caffeine-tainted breast milk.)

We chat congenially, parent to parent. It's comforting. He lightly chides me for not being on more daycare wait lists this late in the game. He commiserates about the torturous lack of sleep. He shows me pictures of his son, and I pull up one of my daughter on my phone.

And then he casually jokes, "So have you been through that phase where you actually think you're going to write about this?"

When I look back on the first year of my daughter's life now, seven years later, I feel like so many of the things I decided to do I did too soon. I was too hard on myself, put too much pressure on myself to be normal, whatever "normal" means.

I wanted so badly to write the way I used to, as often as I used to, about all the things I used to write about—a take on the latest buzzy television show, a takedown of a high-profile sexist comment, a gleeful ode to a slugger's celebratory bat flip—despite how far away those things suddenly felt from my day-to-day experience. And when the words just wouldn't come, when I found that they, like me, were lost in a fog, I tried haplessly to wrestle them out, chastising myself when they weren't perfect. I berated myself for not caring about the things I used to care about, and then twisted and tied myself up in knots to make myself care about them again. I constantly worried that people would forget about me if I no longer produced and published and appeared the way I used to. If I was no longer visible the way I used to be.

Now I know that I was desperately trying to get back to a place that simply didn't exist anymore. Now I don't lament my lack of productivity but instead lament how hard I was on myself—like that day at the university, beating myself up for a stain on my shirt.

When my writer friend asks me in his office if I'm "going to write about this," at first I assume he's being sincere. My daughter is my whole world right now and this casual chat, this flashback to my old life, is merely a small diversion. Tomorrow I will be back on the multicoloured play mat in the living room. Tomorrow I'll be cleaning up spills, pumping breast milk, and playing lullabies on Spotify. I have long used the personal as subject matter, and this all-encompassing experience of bringing a human into the world is something far beyond the personal. I can't keep up with pop culture, or news headlines, or even the latest baseball score, so of course I'm going to write about the single most seismic life change I have ever endured. The abrupt, demoralizing, and transcendent transition to motherhood—the thing that consumes my every thought, every moment of every day.

I mean, what else can I possibly write about?

But after a few beats I can read on his face—in his friendly smirk—that he isn't actually sincere. He isn't actually interested in that messy, shapeless document in which I have been frantically collecting my thoughts on the topic of motherhood as they come to me. The question he is really asking when he asks me if I'm going to write about "this" is *who would ever want to read about that?*

In the moment, sitting across from him, I feel deep embarrassment that I hide with laughter. I think about the near-illegible scrawl in a notebook by my bed, snug in a box that also contains my breast pads and my nipple cream. I think about the fact that our bedroom is littered with notes taken during baby naps—unformed but urgent ideas that are trying to become something if only they could be prioritized. I think about the feeling that I haven't written a good sentence for close to a year and the fact that my phone never rings. I think about that empty inbox. I think about all the people who have told me to "give it time," and how much I desperately want them to tell me *how much time, exactly*.

For four years before my daughter was born, I dealt with infertility. I talked about it rarely and only published one piece of writing about it, despite how much the whole miserable experience consumed my thoughts. Even when I did write about my recurring failure to conceive, I was vague, referring to it in palatable, digestible metaphor. When writing about my miscarriage, I wrote, "I was pregnant and then I was not." I stressed that the pregnancy loss was "very early" and "only happened once" to ensure readers knew it was "not a big deal, really." I even asked the editor who handled the piece if I should take the detail out, out of respect for women who had suffered so much more than I had.

Despite all the chaos, and the pain, and that deep well of grief that infertility carved out of me, I was uncharacteristically composed in print. I was distanced. I was resigned. I was *fine*.

I didn't write about the early-morning visits to the fertility clinic or the iodine that was injected into my fallopian tubes to see if they were blocked. I didn't write about how the painkillers I had taken to endure the procedure had long worn off while I sat for hours in the waiting room, or how I openly wept in pain while the ultrasound technician chided me.

"C'mon. It doesn't hurt that bad," she said as the fluid coursed through my gut and painted the image on her screen. (My fallopian tubes were just fine, the test proved. A brief celebration followed by a shrug. "I guess we still don't know what the issue is, then.")

I didn't write about infertility because it's so hard to write about infertility while it's happening to you. Readers want stories with endings. They want to know that you did everything you could, that you never gave up, and then, because you hoped hard and worked hard and the universe is just, that you got your squirming, squealing, adorable happy ending. They don't want to know that eventually you quit going to the infertility clinic because you simply couldn't take it anymore.

Readers want some sort of resolution to the narrative you've given them. But when you're dealing with infertility, there is no resolution. There is only the seemingly endless cyclical shift back and forth between hope and despair.

And *who would ever want to read about that?*

Despite my embarrassment, it's hard to be mad at my professor friend for his lighthearted derision. After all, the oft-tossed-around joke of writing about motherhood is not a new one. And though fatherhood seems to carry more weight as a "serious literary subject" (think Karl Ove Knausgaard and Michael Chabon), I knew even then that he was speaking from a place of empathy and commiseration. I knew he was mocking his own writerly compulsion to document an experience that billions of people go through.

But in the moment, about to talk to a room full of young people who assume I'm an authority on a subject they care deeply about, I'm red-faced and ashamed. Despite its undeniable importance, the drastic and sometimes even violent shift into motherhood is a subject that seems to lack all seriousness, that fails to interest, that bores to death. It's like describing shopping lists, or your dreams, or the contents of your medicine cabinet. The associated identity shift (and crisis) is so everyday and commonplace as to be meaningless. Certainly not enthralling. Certainly not the subject of respected literature. Certainly not something one would want to spend years of their life writing about (and yes, it has definitely now been years) only to find out no one fucking cares.

Despite the unfathomable, unimaginable depth of this incredible physical, emotional, and spiritual experience, one that splits you in two and opens you up wide, making you question everything you knew about yourself and your world, destroying you while also somehow making you whole—for everyone else it's merely bland blah blah blah minutia.

If I'm honest, the motherhood joke has haunted every page I have written since my daughter's birth.

Writer Rachel Cusk, famous (and infamous) for her own brutally honest accounts of motherhood's relationship to creativity, notes our cultural disdain for motherhood narratives in her essay collection *Coventry*, stating that "the sheer intolerance for these subjects in the twenty-first century is unarguable proof that woman is on the verge of surrendering important aspects of her modern identity." After I had my daughter I came to understand that intolerance is everywhere—a sort of vague disgust that a mother would dare speak about what fills her days, that she would dare to push a stroller down a grocery aisle, or appear in public with a crying baby, or even assume anyone would want to hear her talk about the thing that consumes her entire waking and sleep-deprived life. Motherhood is often oppressively touted as one of the most important things a woman can do, and yet that same oppressive force demands she never speak on the inherent realities of mothering.

It was only later that it would occur to me that it makes no sense that this incredible, miraculous, beautiful, spiritual, elemental, animal experience gets reduced to cookie crumbs, sippy cups, and taking up too much space.

Or maybe it makes perfect sense.

The birth that came after four years of trying and waiting. The birth where I laboured over three calendar days and eventually tore open. The birth that was terrible until it was beautiful. The birth that now belongs to her because the story became hers—became better—the minute she appeared.

My story, an unresolved tragedy of infertility, was no longer mine because she was the narrative climax. My daughter was the narrative climax of a story I was or wasn't telling. She obliterated all the struggle, the scars that came before her, simply by appearing.

So many years after my English professor friend made that innocent, throw-away comment over paper cups of coffee in his office, I still genuinely wonder if anyone will really care about the emotional and physical trauma, the sense of feeling lost, invisible, and adrift in motherhood. I wonder if anyone will care about what it feels like to be cut through and opened by love, and by fear, and by a loss of identity. So everyday as to be meaningless.

It seems to me that we—we being mothers, but also women at large—dismiss our own experiences, our own pain, over and over again. First, we are asked to dismiss it, and then, through time, we dismiss it voluntarily. We say it is not worth mentioning. We excuse it away over and over again, until no one has a right to their own suffering anymore. Our scars sit at a distance from us, just out of reach, proof that a thing has happened, but that it is not wholly ours, ever fading. Becoming invisible.

"She's healthy. That's all that matters," I say after she is born.

"She's healthy. That's all that matters," I say with a messily stitched-up tear.

"She's healthy. That's all that matters," I say when the nurse accidentally drops me on the floor on the way to the bathroom.

"She's healthy. That's all that matters," I say when I can't walk unaided for weeks.

"She's healthy. That's all that matters," I say when I weep in the middle of the night.

The notes I initially took to write this are littered with little scrawled reminders in the margins—things I had to schedule, or buy, or do for my daughter. After I wrote the word "suffering," I made a note about a nameplate I wanted to buy for her bedroom door. After the word "grief," I made a note about how I had to pick up some baby wipes. There is a reminder to book a physiotherapy appointment because so many months (and now years) later, my body is still broken from the physical trauma that I voluntarily dismiss. I haven't healed, and probably never will, but who would want to read about that?

Cookie crumbs, sippy cups, and taking up too much space. Grocery lists, medicine cabinets, and dreams no one really wants to hear about.

I fought so hard not to write about motherhood, bought into the lie of the joke, and I am not sure why. I have delayed it and denied it, pretended it was not necessity. Perhaps it is the voices of literary men, or the anxious voice inside me that asks me to be small and hidden, to pretend it doesn't matter, that it's *no big deal*, that it's *not that bad*.

But the reality is that I have always written about the things that drive me, that preoccupy me, that consume me—and now what is more on my mind every minute of every day than her?

My professor friend and I finished our coffees and our chat, and he took me down the hall to speak to his class of a dozen young hopefuls. It was, of course, as wonderful as I remembered, and despite feeling like a tired, boring imposter in a fog with a baby stain on her shirt, it went just fine. I was pleasantly surprised by the sound of my own voice—almost authoritative, suddenly adult, definitely not singsongy like it was confined to the multicoloured play mat. The students offered thoughtful questions, and I gave honest answers, and to close, one asked me to read aloud from my fourth book, a collection of baseball essays.

I chose the piece about Father's Day at the ballpark, and winkingly dedicated it to my professor friend.

In the time that has passed since that day at the university, I have come to understand that being present as a mother in my creative work is deeply important. Identity is a complicated, shifting beast, and there is no point in denying who I am, or who I have become, or what this new part of me can offer. There is no point in concealing a large chunk of my reality in aid of a system that consistently demands and then devalues that particular chunk. If serious literature—and culture in general—does not want to include the less-celebrated and more-concealed parts of our lives, then what is the point of it at all?

My daughter is in every moment—every small, quiet, intimate thing. She is in all the pieces of me, public and private, lost and found, broken and healed. And she is certainly in the writing. In every word. Despite how much I may have tried to excise her from it. From now on, she will always be in the writing. Sometimes I write for her and sometimes against her, but she is always present.

In those early days and months, I so often lamented that I couldn't write because of her. The truth is I cannot write without her.

Barren

I disliked the fertility doctor immediately.

Of course, given the circumstances, I couldn't exactly have been expected to be happy around him, but he seemed almost smarmy. So judgmental. As if, with his deep breathy sighs and unreadable facial expressions, he was silently cataloguing all the reasons possible—or responsible—for my inexplicable inability to get pregnant.

By that point I didn't need a doctor to convince me that things were entirely my fault—I was already convinced. Maybe it was that flirtation with an eating disorder I had in high school, or the vodka cranberries I had a weekly Thursday-night binge-fling with in university, or those two lines of cocaine I did at a party in an apartment above an art gallery in 2004. (Only ever the two, I promise.)

And now there was a man sitting across from me, a cold professional who was paid to carefully catalogue all those reasons. Gazing at ultrasound images of my uterus on his desk, tapping his ballpoint pen, trying to discern at exactly what point—and by what misstep—it (and consequently I) had become defective.

How many people had I slept with in my twenties? How many meals had I skipped in the pursuit of impossible thinness? How many times had I had that one drink too many? Was I eating whole-fat dairy products and avocados and walnuts like they told me to?

Was I getting enough sleep and avoiding stress? Was I taking my temperature, peeing on the ovulation prediction sticks, and tracking my cycle diligently?

Perhaps most importantly, why had I waited so long to try? Why had I doomed myself to be a *geriatric mother*—an actual term for mothers over thirty-five, by the way—instead of getting pregnant earlier when presumably it would have been easier for everyone involved?

(This was always the hardest line of questioning because the answers were undeniably selfish: I wasn't ready, I wanted to travel, I wanted to work, I wanted to write, I wanted a life of my own before I took care of someone else's. How dare I.)

By the time we ended up in the office of the smarmy, judgmental fertility doctor, my husband and I had been "actively" trying to have a baby for about fourteen months. It would be almost five years after we started trying before we would actually have that baby—torturous years of wondering exactly what I had done wrong, what misguided choices I had made that led me to this miserable place of near-constant yearning, second-guessing, shame, and guilt.

My husband is admirably immune to the judgment of strangers and much less prone to the kind of second-guessing the fertility doctor immediately inspired in me. He tends to be matter-of-fact about the way he has decided to live: his unhealthy lack of sleep, a tendency toward workaholism, a general disinterest in exercise, a joint before bed. He is certainly not without his own set of worries, nor is he beyond self-critique, but he doesn't feel the need to justify himself the way I do, and certainly not to a fertility doctor—a stranger—who we plan to pay for the privilege of providing us with a rather expensive service.

In fact, if I'm honest, my husband is generally better at being human than I am. He is able to relay compliments he's been given without that dismissive embarrassed tone that I often adopt. He is able to be unashamed about who he is and able to feel good about himself without excusing it. He is certainly much better equipped to handle the anxiety of this particular monumental life experience.

(Of course, I admire all of this about him up until the point when it is me who wants his remorse—because he forgot to clean the litter box, because he didn't put away his socks, because he has come home late from work without calling.)

As the poet Lorna Crozier once wrote of her husband Patrick Lane: "This was a man who knew what he wanted and who refused to be ashamed or diverted by the possible outrage of others." I simultaneously feel a sort of admiration mixed with exhausted frustration for this kind of character—how sure he is of exactly who he is, of what he wants, and of what he should do in a way I never will be.

This is not to say my husband hasn't endured anything significant. He has, of course, had a privileged white male life, something that contributes greatly to that ability to convey his worth—but there weren't many at the starting gate who told him how wonderful he was, that his choices were good and valid and entirely his. He was by some definitions neglected and as a result became incredibly self-sufficient. His self-confidence seems to have grown out of a terrible, not-often-discussed necessity—sure of himself despite where he started, not because of it.

In the context of our "infertility journey" (a phrase strewn across social media and chat forums that I will grow to both lean on and despise), this self-confidence and lack of personal excuses manifests in some helpful, no-nonsense ways. He has no issue disclosing his marijuana use to the smarmy fertility doctor and asserting that he will "in no way give it up ever" (his words exactly). Even when the doctor informs him this is probably not the best choice, he basically says he doesn't care. For him, marijuana is a medical necessity in the face of his chronic insomnia (caused by aforementioned workaholism, naturally). It's not even that he's making excuses. He knows himself well enough to know that regardless of any arguments, things would be much worse without it. (And for what it's worth, I agree, and the test results assured us his daily joint was not a problem.)

My husband doesn't feel the burden of blame for our infertility like I do. That may have something to do with the built-in attributes that guide how each of us sees the world, but I am more apt to think this is gendered. Regardless of evidence, our culture likes to blame women when their bodies won't produce a desired child. And no matter how many possible reasons the fertility doctor manages to come up with to put in his growing catalogue, I will always be able to list more in the blame centre of my mind. I am always being mythically punished for some prior bad act or indiscretion. We haven't established whose "fault" it actually is (no one's, it will turn out), but it is so very obviously mine. I don't deserve to be a mother.

The fertility doctor tells me about the vials of blood they will draw, the tests they will do, the things they will inject, the pictures they will take of my misbehaving parts. He lists off the procedures that could follow, in ascending order of invasiveness. (It is not lost on me that most of the "internal" work would fall to me, while my husband's role would be largely "external.")

The doctor then tells us about our chances, but I've stopped listening.

In my mind all my bad decisions, all my selfish behaviours have brought me to this terrible place, sitting across from this man who taps his pen absentmindedly on an ultrasound of my uterus, cataloging my flaws beneath the weight of his breathy sighs.

By the time I was diagnosed with "unexplained infertility" in early 2015, I had been doing a hell of a lot of hoping. That hope was the very thing that made finding out that I wasn't pregnant, month after month after month, so acutely painful.

All the well-meaning platitudes that friends and family delivered when they found out we were "trying," all the advice they gave, all the anecdotes they thoughtfully but uselessly relayed—about how I just had to relax and be patient, that there was "a baby out there for me," that my turn would come; about how "trying was the fun part," how all I really had to do was drink a great deal of tequila—were exactly what made the years without any good news so debilitating.

Experts recommend that if you are under the age of thirty-five, you should see a fertility specialist after a year of trying with no success. I was approaching my thirty-sixth birthday when I ended up across the desk from the judgmental man with his list of invasive questions, definitely feeling like I should have addressed my failures sooner.

During those years, infertility created this pervasive, insidious hum of disappointment in my life, a yearning that lingered like a malevolent ghost in the background. It made me feel outside myself looking in. The inability to conceive transformed me into something simultaneously invisible and grossly exposed, as if I was meaningless because I was "childless," and publicly ashamed because my body was faulty. (Neither of those awful, self-punishing ideas was true, of course, but as much as you tell them to go away, they pound endlessly on the door, demanding to be let in.)

I started frequenting message boards online and on the apps I downloaded to carefully track my fertility, referring to them as "the place where hope goes to die." Would-be mothers shared tips and tricks along with their own personal misery, publicly praying to Jesus and posting "TMI!" photos of their cervical mucus, querying the masses about whether or not the consistency suggested a fertile window. (When you try for a long time to have a baby, you become a bit of a cervical mucus expert.) Initially it felt easy to mock these women, with their earnest, cutesy euphemisms for sex ("the baby dance") and acronyms like AF ("Aunt Flow") or BFN ("Big Fat Negative," as in pregnancy test), but soon it all just made me feel sad—the cyclical disappointment, the candid confessions of jealousy, the general hopelessness.

Unsurprisingly, I hated Mother's Day during those terrible years. I avoided mentions of it, logged off when I could, and tried to turn away from the relentless, bright-pink celebration of it all. In my work as a sports writer, I would occasionally have to write fluffy yet moving pieces about baseball players and their devoted moms, so I put on a brave face, just as I did when I expelled platitudes wishing happiness to everyone who celebrated. In truth I hated watching the players in their pink-accented hats and jerseys, hated their pink bats and cleats. I hated the in-stadium promotions, concourse spa treatments, the mom-appropriate giveaways.

More than anything else, I hated the empty sentiment that being a mother is "the most important job in the world," and hated my own desperate wanting to be the recipient of that empty sentiment. I hated how miserable the vital celebration of motherhood made me, hated being reminded of what I couldn't have, hated being destroyed by someone else's good news.

I even started to hate my own hate.

A baby was my dream, and I filled that absence with another dream. Baseball saved me from sadness in both work and life. During the years I struggled with infertility, the game of baseball was the perhaps frivolous—but also professional—distraction that filled the deep silence of my failure to conceive. I waited many seasons for my daughter to become more than just a wish, and during that time I found solace in the game's distractions and hope in its meaning. I've come to understand that in a strange way, its players were like my children when I couldn't have one of my own.

I tracked my cycle via the game. I remembered my ovulation schedule like I remembered the Toronto Blue Jays' home and away games, remembered I had been menstruating when the Yankees were in town, or that I was due to when the Jays played the first game of a series in Boston. In 2015, the year I was diagnosed with "unexplained infertility," my team and their schedule did an excellent job of distracting me from the inevitable abyss of "what ifs" and "when?"

The Blue Jays' increasing success from spring to summer of that year blotted out more fatalistic thoughts and consistently gave me something to look forward to. Despite how isolated I felt, despite feeling like I wasn't allowed to talk about what I was enduring, I could go to a Sunday afternoon game, take in nine innings and a few beers, and feel decidedly less alone. I could escape into a community of frenzied fans and feel part of something larger than my worries. I could submerge myself in something so very far removed from any genuine conversations about motherhood, something that never concerned itself with the ceaseless woes of infertility.

When I made the difficult decision to quit my full-time magazine job in the interest of reducing that stress that everyone kept citing as a fertility problem, more consistent freelance writing about baseball gratefully filled my days, and silenced the nagging worry that I would never become a mother.

When the dog days of summer hit, the Toronto Blue Jays looked like genuine contenders for the first time in decades. After taking a ballpark road trip to California in late July, where I watched the Jays win a three-game series against the Oakland A's, I maintained my immovable faith in both my chances of conceiving and my team, and kept a keen eye on both arduous cycle tracking and the standings.

I returned to Toronto to watch newly signed David Price's glorious pitching debut at Rogers Stadium with the knowledge that

I was finally late. I stood in the stands with my hand on my belly, surrounded by thousands of others also deliriously stricken by hope, and I couldn't help but selfishly think the baseball gods were finally rewarding me for my devotion.

A few days late. A few weeks late.

And then it was over.

I was pregnant and then I was not.

I had a *very early* miscarriage in mid-August and was amazed by how numb I was to that brief life and its abrupt end, the blood and the pain and my small hope extinguished. It was as if, after so many months of trying, I couldn't be convinced of the idea of having a child anyway. Disappointment seemed an obvious result. A miracle—a tiny life—did not. Just another thing to track on the calendar.

Like so many traumatic things that came before it, that week in August now exists like a thumbprint smudge in my memory, something made blurry because I don't want to look at it ever again. Because I need to be protected from it.

Move forward, I remember thinking. *Forget.*

Whatever personal failure I felt that late summer was soothed by my baseball team's sudden surge of success and all the public joy that surrounded it. The game had taught me to bounce back after setbacks and disappointments. It had taught me there'd always be another day. It had taught me about hope.

But it wasn't the team's turn that year, and it wasn't mine either. That was what I told myself over and over to endure it. I was in the stands with my hand on my belly and then it was over. It was over and forgotten.

(It was never forgotten.)

The woman who lives across the street from me was pregnant again, her second pregnancy in less than two years.

I was happy for her. I really was.

I watched from my front window as she descended the steps of her two-storey house, all swollen and glowing, clutching the pudgy hand of her barely walking toddler as the two of them—the three of them—wandered to the corner store to pick up a few things.

It seems the women on my street, so many of them young and newly married, get pregnant so easily, so quickly. We congratulate them and coo over their new babies, count ourselves lucky to have so many adorable children to decorate our sidewalks with chalk drawings and collect up our peanut-free candy at Halloween.

Of course I am happy for them, but there is also a part of me that is crazy with jealousy, angry that it seems so easy for them when I had to sit across from the smarmy doctor and answer his invasive questions.

This is an irrational ache—I know this—but still, selfishly, I don't want to hear their happy news. It is the same irrational feeling that prompts me to mute people on social media after I am confronted with their pregnancy announcements.

I rarely wrote about infertility while it was happening to me, and I regret that now. At the time the suffering felt far too private, the wound far too raw to share with anyone else. In some ways it still does feel that way. But in my quiet misery I did seek out authentic stories to heal me, hungered for the knowing looks and words of women who had endured what I was enduring and who had fought their way through, women who were still fighting and simply living. Something beyond all the judgment. Something that treated the whole messy issue with the sensitivity and kindness it necessitated.

Imagine knowing that holding out hope is the very thing that's keeping you from healing. Imagine knowing the minute you let go is the minute you might start to feel better. Imagine refusing to let go for years and years.

In a *New York Times* piece titled "The Lasting Trauma of Infertility," Regina Townsend, founder of *The Broken Brown Egg* blog, writes: "Because it can be hard to fully grasp what infertility involves unless you've dealt with it personally, many people believe that it's all about the end game, a baby—that if you could just get to that prize, the pain of infertility would fade away. But infertility is bigger than babies." (She adds that research has shown women dealing with infertility have depression and anxiety levels similar to those with cancer, HIV, and heart disease.)

"You become used to living in a constant state of fluctuating despair and hope," Townsend continues. "And this doesn't turn off when and if you get pregnant. It doesn't turn off when you hear or see the heartbeat. My son is 3. I'm still trying to turn it off."

There are so many of us trying to turn it off.

So often we talk about letting go of being a victim, of not letting what has destroyed you, month after month, come to define you. But who was I when those layers of grief and loss were pulled away? Who was I beyond the victim of my body's own inability to give me what I longed for? What was left of me other than the fact that my body had failed?

As pregnancy test after pregnancy test came back negative, I wrote constantly. I wrote hundreds of pieces about movies, books, sports, current events, my life, and other people's lives. I reviewed television shows, rounded up the hottest summer reads, and dissected the feminist implications of the latest frothy blockbuster.

I wrote magazine features, incendiary opinion columns, a weekly newsletter, and, in less than a year, an entire book about the game I loved. I wrote things that resulted in virulent hate mail and the occasional not-so-veiled personal threat. I wrote to prove myself in a male-dominated industry, for publications that paid me very little and very late, and in some cases for editors who paid me very little respect. I wrote myself into demand, which is simply how this business works—never turn down an assignment, never say no for fear that it will be the last time someone asks. I wrote until I was completely exhausted, occasionally having a quiet cry at my desk because of the sheer volume of words I had committed to and the anxiety of having to put them out into the world on a deadline.

"I can do it," I said, even if it was impossible.

During that extremely difficult time, I very intentionally worked myself numb, salving the trauma of infertility with the convenient distraction of labour—some of which I of course loved and felt lucky to do, but a lot of which brought me even more stress, misery, and deep bone-tiredness. I was living in fear that if I stopped the momentum, I would be alone with my own thoughts, alone with the very real possibility I would never be a mother.

In retrospect, it was an entirely unhealthy way to deal with the sad lot of childlessness I felt like I had been given, but it was the only way of coping I could think of that wasn't more stereotypically self-destructive—instead of consuming intoxicants alone in the dark, I was being paid and applauded in the light. I was doing exactly what my culture and community had asked of me, exactly what it viewed as personal success. I was invited to high-profile events. I was invited to write columns. I was invited to comment on things, even if I didn't feel qualified to do so, as if my viewpoint mattered in a way it never had before.

In a privately dismal period of my life, I felt publicly loved, however hollow and faulty that love really was, never realizing that love could disappear as quickly as it arrived.

Every time I would find out I wasn't pregnant—whether via a rush of blood and dull pain or a disappointing pregnancy test—I would take myself out. More often than not I would sneak away from my desk and slip a book into my purse, going to lunch alone at the

Museum Tavern. I would eat a Cobb salad and drink a glass of Riesling, languishing at the bar in that worry-less way only people without children can.

I would sit there, in the perfect company of strangers, and think about the life I could have without a child: impromptu travel during the school year, dinners without babysitters, general freedom. I would think about how of course I could find happiness without the baby I so wanted, how my life was just fine as it was, even with the relentless ache of that piece that was missing.

On those terrible days I discovered I wasn't pregnant (again, and again, and again), I would sometimes take myself to the museum, or the art gallery, and look at all the endless devotional depictions of mother and child. Like some kind of bizarre exposure therapy, I would torture myself with their blissful repose and placid expressions, berating myself with the beauty of it all. Sitting quietly, perfectly still on a bench facing the product of immaculate conception, I would take in the bold primary colours of vivid stained glass or the time-faded brush strokes of an elated Madonna, her beloved pudgy messiah at her exposed breast.

Sometimes, while I sat there in the warm light of the museum, I would rationalize. Sometimes I would cry. Sometimes I would simply be reserved, or resigned. It was a kind of monthly grief, unrecognized and unseen, without any kind of road map. It was a narrative I was writing alone because—despite how many women endure it—it so often felt like no one had ever written it before.

I was twelve years old when the 1992 American psychological thriller *The Hand That Rocks the Cradle* was released. Hugely popular at the time, the movie tells the story of "good mother" Claire

Bartel and a psychopathic, vengeful nanny named Peyton who finds her way into her home. Unbeknownst to Claire, Peyton blames her for the loss of her own baby and subsequent hysterectomy, and endeavours to destroy Claire's picture-perfect happy picket-fence life by turning her entire family against her—new baby included.

I was thoroughly entertained. I never thought to question this grotesque—and frankly lazy—idea of "infertile, childless woman as villain," perhaps because by that point she was already embedded in my consciousness. Culturally, the woman who cannot (or doesn't want to) have children is commonly viewed as broken, or misguided, or even monstrous in some fundamental way. The childless and childfree have been villainous in plenty a children's fairy tale, making it not much of a pop culture leap to have the new nanny vengefully breastfeeding the good mother's child, seducing the good mother's husband, murdering the good mother's best friend, or covertly emptying all the good mother's asthma inhalers.

The Hand That Rocks the Cradle is an extreme and, yes, laughable example, but after years of dealing with infertility and loss, it's hard not to view Peyton and her pathological nature as a cautionary tale. If your journey to motherhood fails, if it is unsuccessful or meets a tragic end, you too will become the bad guy in the good mother narrative. You'll be the witch woman, the creepy crone at the far edge of the playground, staring longingly at other people's children. Your bitterness, your resentment, your jealousy over pregnant bellies on the subway or in the grocery store will make you a shell of your former, hopeful self.

You will single-mindedly hate other people's happiness. You will never find peace.

None of these things are true, of course. But when Peyton is eventually thrown from the attic window by the virtuous mother and violently impaled on the good family's aforementioned white picket fence, we are certainly made to fear a childless fate. And when the sight of someone else's pregnancy announcement fills you with misplaced resentment and something resembling rage, it's not hard to see yourself as the monster pop culture has already suggested you are.

I once told a friend that the experience of infertility was like a grief over something you've lost but never known—a grief that won't end until you finally give up the hope of ever knowing it.

I mean, how many times, how many months, how many years can you miss a hypothetical child, a child that you cannot have, before that need destroys you? How long can you live with feelings no one else understands or acknowledges, that you yourself cannot articulate, that you mostly hide because that's easier than explaining? How many times can you take yourself out for a glass of wine and a Cobb salad, to the museum or art gallery, before you decide this punishing path is and will forever be fruitless? How long before you finally turn away from motherhood and toward something that feels possible?

How long before you have to move on, if you can?

There are phenomena that experts call disenfranchised grief and ambiguous grief. Essentially, disenfranchised grief is caused by a loss not acknowledged by society, suffered in silence and isolation, and ambiguous grief is caused by a loss unresolved, something that others are not sure really exists but you know to be true. "Ambiguous losses are a particular type of loss that is hard to define and lacks closure," says Dr. Kelly Maxwell Haer in an interview for Ada Calhoun's book *Why We Can't Sleep: Women's New Midlife Crisis*. "That hope lingers on and it's hard to live in hope that is not met. It's not like the closure of death where you know this person has died, and it's over, and you can go through grief and move on. Humans don't do uncertainty well."

These concepts go a long way in explaining the grief I felt as each unsuccessful month came and went—not acknowledged, not perceived to be true, certainly with no closure or resolution, but so entirely mine to mourn.

Because mourning is so important to healing, infertility left me with an open wound—vulnerable month after month, season after season, year after year. I often wonder what I could have done, over those four years, with all the energy that went into my pain. I wonder what I could have made, or learned, or given to the world. What I could have created if I wasn't sitting at the bar, grieving into my Riesling.

What shape does grief take when it isn't acknowledged? Is it worn like a coat? Does it make us feel unseen, swallow us up, or steal from us without us even realizing it? How can we carry it around for so long without falling apart?

By the time winter started to thaw in 2017, I was in my late thirties and the genuine despair of not being able to have a baby was taking its toll. My husband and I had seen multiple specialists, traditional and otherwise, and had been subjected to invasive questions, testing, and procedures. After years of losing ourselves to the process, we mutually decided to take a break, wanting to breathe and focus on our well-being.

The answer to how long you can endure hoping before you have to move on was answered. Despite how much I desperately wanted a child, how much that want consumed all my thoughts and days, I was coming to the end.

In our fourth year of trying to have a baby, on Easter weekend, a rabbit showed up on our front lawn.

It was my neighbour who spotted the impossibly fluffy creature first, finding it nestled in the grass while she was on a walk around the neighbourhood. She gingerly scooped up the bunny, wrapped it in a worn baby-blue bath towel, and, along with a comical chunk of carrot, placed it in an oversized clear plastic bin. She then walked it up my steps and rang my doorbell.

"Is this your rabbit?" she asked—probably the funniest question anyone has ever asked while at my front door. (It was, of course, not my rabbit.)

Bright-white, freckled with pale-grey spots, and featuring an adorably twitchy pink nose, this was very likely someone's rabbit. Barring a small tear in his very upright right ear—what I assumed was the result of a neighbourhood cat—the bunny was entirely clean. Pristine. Very household pet-like.

It turned out my neighbour was going away that weekend and unable to care for this newly acquired orphan. Besides, the bunny had decided to take up residence on my lawn, and because of that I felt a genuine sense of responsibility. As a person who already had three rescued animals inside, it was predictable I'd volunteer to take care of this stranger—at least for a day or two.

Most people who foster stray animals understand the process usually involves a promise of a "few days until we can figure something out," and then those days multiply into something a lot more meaningful.

That's how a rabbit came to live in our home the spring our daughter was finally conceived.

The first weekend the orphan bunny stayed with us, we tried our best to spread the word through various channels that we'd found him. Given how adorable he was, surely there was someone out there missing him dearly. Surely there was a crying child hoping he'd come home, a parent frantically drying those tears while reporting the loss to animal services. They would of course be scouring the internet for any "FOUND RABBIT" updates, looking for posters affixed to lampposts.

In the meantime, we gave the rabbit his own bedroom. We moved our dog's old crate from the basement into the spare room next to ours, filling it with soft worn blankets and a sweet specialty hay I found at the local pet food store. I lovingly fed him lettuce, spinach, and kale by hand. I peeled him bananas and watched him nibble away at them while he sat on my lap. I would let him bounce around on my bed while I read books, wrote, or watched TV. I would cradle him like a baby and stroke his tiny head while he twitched.

As the weeks wore on, no one responded to our postings, but lots of people came to visit, each wanting an opportunity to hold the rabbit in the crook of their arm and scratch gently between his ears. He was skittish but generally enjoyed the attention, eventually relaxing into their chests as they held him close. A handful of these people even kindly offered to adopt him, but each had to back out at the last moment—a partner with an allergy, an impending trip, a fear of too much responsibility.

I learned a lot about rabbits during the time our visitor came to stay. I learned that this bunny was indeed a domestic—a Rex to be specific: a plush, velvety breed that originated in France in 1919. I learned that it's very common for rabbits like him to be abandoned, especially around Easter when they're procured for amusement and then simply "let go."

I learned that rabbits are community-minded creatures—they live in tightly knit groups—and that the instinctual thumping they do with their back legs is a way to warn the rest of the warren of danger. I learned that last fact because, despite how safe and comforting I tried to make this rabbit's world, how badly I wanted him to stay, the two cats and a dog that also called my house home terrified him.

That spring I also learned that the rabbit is a symbol of prosperity, abundance, and, of course, fertility.

As the weeks wore on, it became increasingly clear that no matter how many tweets we tweeted or photocopied posters we hung, no one was coming to claim our furry visitor as their lost pet. He was very likely abandoned, an idea that, because of my fragile state, wounded me more than it should have. After delaying his departure as long as we could, and after lots of kale, spinach, and bananas, we finally spoke to a west end animal rescue about finding our rabbit friend a more accommodating forever home.

On a cool Saturday morning in May, we reluctantly passed our bunny along to a pair of kindly elderly women who arranged the adoption, struggling to say goodbye as we scratched one more time between those upright ears.

It's funny how you develop a quick affection for things that were never really yours, how you fall in love with ideas, lives you could have lived, even if you can't have them yourself.

As much as I wanted to keep the rabbit, as much as it hurt to fold up the crate and sweep the hay from the spare bedroom, it also felt good to have temporarily taken him in, to have given him a safe home until a new and better one came along. If anything, the rabbit had given me a break from all those thoughts that I couldn't shake, a reprieve from my constant yearning, a place to put my attention and care.

And within a week of letting go and saying goodbye, I was pregnant. After about forty-five months of trying and failing and trying again, I was pregnant.

I was finally going to have a baby.

When my doctor called to confirm the news, I was overjoyed but found it hard to breathe a sigh of relief and celebrate. I kept waiting for some disaster to befall me. I anxiously endured those first three months, telling only a few people out of fear of early miscarriage. I spent that time holding my secret close, worrying over every scheduled test, checking daily as my chance of loss statistically decreased, and vomiting just about anywhere and everywhere. I had gotten what I always wanted and there I was, so terrified to lose it I couldn't even enjoy it.

Cautiously wading into the safety of the second trimester, I began to settle in and proceed with the idea that, yes, I would finally become a mother. I started to buy all those tiny, adorable outfits and pick out things for the nursery. (My first purchase was made around the seventeen-week mark: a jersey-style onesie from the Toronto Blue Jays in-stadium shop that I laid out on our bed and stared at for a good fifteen minutes.)

After many excruciating months of salving my disappointment, I felt like I was living in a dream world. Far worse was that I was sure I would wake up from said dream. I was waiting for the other shoe to drop, certain something tragic would happen to take away all this perfect joy, so much so that, in some misguided plan not to tempt fate, I refused to even feel it.

Turns out that having a baby didn't mean I had suddenly healed from the trauma of infertility. Instead, I carried that familiar monthly swell of grief into my pregnancy and well into my daughter's life, manifested as a pervasive fear of losing her, and disbelief that she was even here, and real, and mine. The grief had been so much a part of my day-to-day, so much a part of who I was for so long, that I couldn't let it go.

Infertility gives you a lot of time to dream of the future, and prompts you to longingly torture yourself with imaginings of what kind of mother you might be—and what kind of mother you don't want to be. I knew I didn't want to be the kind of mother who was anxious and afraid all the time. I didn't want to worry to the point where I was incapable of enjoying my baby. Even if I couldn't be "good" at motherhood—a word I have since learned is meaningless in this context—I wanted to at least try to learn how to be relaxed, light and carefree. I wanted to learn how to be an easygoing kind of mother, and person, one who could bend with moments and laugh at small disasters and keep moving forward without the grip of terror that a tragedy was awaiting us.

I didn't want to always think something bad was going to happen, like I had for most of my life. I didn't want to miss out on all this promised happiness, this happiness I had longed for, because I was so afraid of losing it. I wanted to keep hoping, even if sometimes it hurt so much to do so.

"Maybe the bad thing already happened," a friend eventually said.

Maybe I had already gotten through the bad thing. Maybe there was no other shoe to drop.

My daughter now sleeps in the same room that stray rabbit lived in during the spring she was conceived.

Sometimes when she wakes up in the middle of the night, I hold her body tight to mine, feeling that ache I had all those years without her. The grief I carried with me for so long lingers, like I am still healing that open wound that left me so vulnerable. Like I am missing her even though she's right here in my arms, the once ever-present longing haunting me like a ghost.

But while the grief of infertility remains even now, so does the hope I refused to let go of through all those disappointing, painful years without her. It was that hope that kept me open-hearted despite my hurt, that allowed me to shelve my rage and resentment and be grateful and caring, that invited possibility despite my desire to simply shut down. It turns out hope did not cause my grief, but helped me endure it. It's what kept me looking to a future, believing that things maybe could and would get better—no matter what that future ended up looking like.

I'm not sure I believe in magic, omens, or good luck charms, but when I hold my daughter close in the middle of the night, I know I believe in hope.

Like a Branch from a Tree in a Storm

A child is born, and funeral bells ring.
You make a little life, and you make a little death too.
—Katrina Onstad, *Stay Where I Can See You*

On an unseasonably warm day in February 2018, my body simply refused to do what it was supposed to.

There had been comprehensive plans and desired outcomes. There had been so many books read and procedures studied. There had been supplies acquired, bags diligently packed, and questions asked in stuffy hospital classrooms on weekend afternoons. Methodologies were thoughtfully debated, and doctrines accepted or refused. But like so many times before this one, my body resisted. And like so many times before this one, it was threatened with force.

When we arrived at the hospital in the early hours the complications were established. First was the risk of meconium aspiration syndrome, something that occurs when a baby breathes a mixture of meconium and amniotic fluid into the lungs around the time of delivery (and a leading cause of severe illness and death in newborns, something I thankfully didn't know at the time). Second, she was what they called "posterior," or adorably nicknamed "sunny-side up," a riskier fetal position where she was facing my stomach and not my back—more common with overdue babies and older moms. Because of these details specialists would be on call, and she would have to be turned, and turned, and turned again.

She couldn't make the journey "normally." She had to be helped along.

"She's drifting to the left," the smiling nurses and doctors told me, as if she was a small boat out on the sea, a little too far from shore, pulling slightly off course.

(A boat pulling off course is certainly not to blame for being off course.)

During every one of those twenty-seven hours I was in labour, I was convinced it was my body's fault that things were complicated. Like most women—mothers, women who can't be mothers, women who don't want to be mothers—the problem was with my body. It needed to be altered, or fixed, or sacrificed. It needed to be better, or more obedient, something other than what it was. It needed to do what it was told.

There was no reason to expect that unseasonably warm day in February to be any different.

What do we mean when we say a birth is "difficult"?

Is it difficult if the mother is pried open, or cut open, or torn open? Is it difficult if someone has to intervene, if there is risk, or if there is the possibility of failure? Is it difficult if the mother catches poorly concealed looks of concern—or worse, *fear*—on the faces of the nurses and doctors that hover above her heaving body?

Is her body—and the fact that it simply won't do what it's supposed to—the thing that makes the birth difficult? Is the birth difficult because she herself is difficult—a difficult body? Ultimately, is she the one who is to blame?

(This may not actually matter, given she will always blame herself.)

I've come to learn the word "difficult" is nothing more than a euphemism, a dismissal, a way of not actually talking about wrongdoings that transpired. It is a convenient way of not looking directly at each of the things that contributed to what eventually became traumatic: the fingers and hands inside me without consent, the drugs denied or administered without discussion.

The doctor or nurse didn't ask permission the first time—and then the second, and then the third, until all those tiny transgressions come to mean there are no boundaries left. I am just a body on a table, nothing but a line between them and a baby. A line that eventually needs to be crossed.

It is easier to submit than protest. The body would say yes to anything if it was afraid enough.

One afternoon when I was in my mid-twenties, while working in administration at a program for people with long-term mental health issues, I was suddenly consumed by the very real and immediate fear that I was dying. Covered in sweat, nauseous and disoriented, I found I could barely stand and ended up collapsing on the floor of the office bathroom after locking myself inside. I called a cab and somehow managed to pull myself into it, getting myself home and into bed until the feeling subsided.

That was the first full-scale panic attack of what would become a suffocating cascade of severe and seemingly insurmountable anxiety symptoms—irrational worries about my health, my job, and my current relationships; fear of the outside world; difficulties sleeping, eating, and making even minor connections with other people.

I became textbook agoraphobic. I could no longer go to the theatre or the movies or a concert, couldn't ride in elevators or on subways, and declined invitations to events and parties. I was fatigued, generally fuzzy-headed, and largely incapable of going beyond the lawn outside my apartment building. If I did leave, I needed a prescription bottle snug in my purse like Dumbo the elephant needed his magic feather.

My body had betrayed me. It had refused to do what it was supposed to do. It was to blame.

That period of severe, housebound anxiety was a pit I eventually climbed out of via the help of my friends and family, a very gifted cognitive behavioural therapist, and the occasional refill of Lorazepam, but I was never the same after that. I was now, officially and enduringly, *an anxious person*. I was afraid of enclosed spaces, the dentist, PAP tests, failure, and the idea that maybe everyone hated me. Despite ongoing therapy and conscious efforts at general wellness, I could never really completely relax, or enjoy the moment. I needed to plan a route that didn't involve the subway, to sit in an aisle seat near the exit, to avoid crowded spaces in general, lest I feel trapped and once again descend into the potential panic that always lurked around the edges of my life. People knew to handle me with kid gloves, to ask me if I was okay, to accommodate me, even to pity me.

People knew I was *difficult*.

And then, more than a decade later, my difficult, anxious, pitied body became a pregnant body.

After I got pregnant something unexpected happened—I started to feel powerful. I think that power had less to do with the usual worn-out clichés of creating and carrying a life and more to do with something far more literal.

My body was getting bigger. I was taking up more space. People were making room for me.

When I was small, men told me they admired my frailty. That they enjoyed the way I fit into the spaces that they made with their bodies, the vacant spots in their big lives. That they enjoyed the knowledge they could overpower me.

Men I loved who became the men who harmed me, the men who violated me.

"You're so small," one once said hungrily as he put his palm on my exposed hip, like he had suddenly and gleefully discovered that he had the ability to crush me like a tiny bird beneath his hand.

And yet when I was pregnant, while so many were treating me like something vulnerable—kindly surrendering their seats, carrying my things, opening doors—I felt paradoxically aggressive and hulking. As my baby grew, my thighs became meaty and firm to support her weight, to the point where I felt like I could easily kick in all those doors that were being held open. Despite my delicate public status, I knew I was gathering strength.

All those years I was terrified of routine appointments and standard medical tests, and now I was rolling through countless blood draws, ultrasounds, and general obstetric prodding with renewed, clear-eyed purpose. Where once I tamped down and severed myself from my emotions, now I was happily wading through them neck deep. (During a trip to the mall, my husband stared in amused confusion as I wept over how beautiful and transcendent Guns N' Roses' "November Rain" was as it played on the car radio.)

The world around me, in all its messiness, noisiness, and hatefulness, faded from view. Within my own tiny sphere, there was a necessity to being present and more focused than ever. And while pregnancy certainly comes with its own unique set of valid worries, my usual nagging ones were dulled, replaced with clarity of purpose I hadn't experienced before.

For the first time in my adult life, instead of loathing and punishing my physical self, I loved getting ready for the day, loved looking at myself in the mirror. I loved my body and everything it could do.

You would think the idea of labour, with its genuine well-established risks, would have brought me anxiety, but two things about it quieted my usually panicked mind: its utter inevitability and the fact that, one way or another, it would eventually end.

Intoxicated by this new feeling of clarity, heft, and purpose, a protective calm enveloped me. For so much of my life I had been something so shrinking and small, a tiny bird pressed beneath the palm of a man's hand. Now I was sure, and solid, and heavy-footed, relishing in growth and momentum.

In the weeks before my daughter was born, the temperature lingered in the minus double digits, so cold that Shelby, our geriatric German Shepherd mix, slept under the covers in our bed, curled up tight against my hugely pregnant and largely immobile body. Swaddled in sweaters and unable to sleep, I would listen to her noisy canine snores as my baby kicked through the night and my due date disappeared behind us.

All the books I diligently read alluded to complications and even stillbirth with overdue babies. As she did with most scary things, my seasoned obstetrician mentioned the various risks in the most casual way possible. And so, in the ten days after I was due, in between a series of unnerving precautionary ultrasounds, watching Hallmark movies, and eating baked goods of all kinds, I did a number of absurd things in the interest of provoking labour.

I took yoga classes where I spent most of the hour simply lying on my mat. I did acupuncture and inhaled the not-so-delicious smell of clary sage. I bounced endlessly on a birthing ball and drank litres of fresh pineapple juice. I walked endless laps around the mall and climbed as many flights of stairs in its parking garage as my body and belly would allow. I even prepared a famed eggplant parmesan recipe published online by a restaurant in Georgia called Scalini's. (A Good Morning America article claims that "more than 300 of the pregnant women customers who ordered the eggplant have given birth within 48 hours," and the restaurant's website boasts dozens of pictures of its "Eggplant Babies.")

All this in the hope that my daughter would safely make her way into the world and I would get some much-needed physical relief. It was very cold, my baby was very overdue, and I was very pregnant.

When none of my tactics for going into labour seemed to be working, I reluctantly submitted to scheduling the induction I really didn't want. A balloon would be inflated in my cervix and left there until my body acquiesced; a Pitocin drip would be hooked up to my arm to "nudge" things along.

The night before that ominous morning appointment, I ate a bowl of yogourt and granola while watching *Jurassic World* in bed. Around the moment Claire Dearing bravely gets Paddock 9 unlocked and sets Tyrannosaurus rex free, my daughter decided it was time.

I can't watch that scene now without crying.

People love to casually ask how your birth experience was. What they really want to hear you say is, *The doctors and nurses did such a good job, she's healthy, that's all that matters, I'm so grateful.*

It took me a long time to say out loud that mine was "you know, *difficult*." It took even longer to say it was traumatic, and even longer still to truly believe that it was. When I told people what happened during my daughter's birth, when I told them how long it took, the risks, and the fears, I would scan their faces for any look that would validate what I was feeling.

"But what counts as a difficult birth?" I would really be asking them as I rattled off all the details.

There are so many horror stories to compare your own against, so many ways you're made to feel lucky instead of hurt, or harmed, or in need of help, that for a long time I felt like my experience—and my need—didn't measure up. I often wondered exactly how many things needed to go wrong before I would qualify for concern, before the curious would also ask me if I was doing okay.

I'm so broken, but so grateful.

It took a long time to say the thing I needed to say. It took the reassuring words of subsequent care providers. It took more books, conversations, and rejected doctrines. It took a period of healing, talking, and thinking about what it truly means to be upended, invaded, violated.

The question *how bad was it?* is a shadow that has followed me most of my life—this terrible, nagging query of how bad a thing needs to be for someone to actually care. Is there a number assigned? A scale of severity? Was the trauma actually in the facts or merely in your reaction to the facts?

How bad was it, really? Is it bad enough to cry about? To talk about? To write about?

Prove it, the world would always seem to say—show us all your available evidence, your darkest fears and most troubled days. Show us your messy feelings, your visible and invisible scars, and then we will decide. Write everything down and put it out there for prying eyes and dirty hands to rummage through, and we will tell you if what you've endured at the hands of others is really bad enough for us to care.

And like so many women speaking of their personal traumatic experiences, I was always tempted to say it was "not that bad."

It was simply easier than calling it what it was.

Unsurprisingly, the man who enjoyed that I was like a bird beneath his palm didn't listen when I said no. When I tried to wriggle free from beneath him, he accused me of being *fucking dramatic*. Of being a difficult body.

They always do that. They do that before, when you refuse, and they do that during, when you protest, and they do that after, when you cry.

I remember he told me not to be so emotional, told me to

fucking relax. Maybe he didn't actually say *fucking* but my mind remembers it that way, as if the aggression of his profanity makes my claim of violation more valid.

As if him swearing at me makes him a monster and not just a man.

The bright light of the huge digital clock on the wall read 12:07 a.m., glowing red in the view between my knees after they pulled her from my body. Her birth certificate says 12:06, but I only remember 12:07. Stunned into immobility, it took me a minute to finally look up.

She was no more than a few seconds old and instead of giving her to me they took her away to a tray on the other side of the large delivery room. They had to make sure she didn't need to go directly to the NICU, and there wasn't any time to discuss it.

(There had actually been hours and hours and hours of time to discuss it.)

She was only about eight feet away for approximately six minutes but it felt like oceans of space and time. After four years of trying to conceive, twenty-seven hours of labour, four hours of pushing, she was finally here. When I was pregnant I could never become comfortable with the fact she was real, and for months and years to come I would be afraid she would simply disappear. This beautiful child who had proved to me that the traumatized body could also be powerful—something more than broken. This otherworldly being who for a long and difficult time I thought would never be.

And they just took her away.

I remember I asked over and over again if she was okay, my voice hoarse, breathless, and pleading. Even though there were suddenly so many people in the room, it felt as if no one would address me directly, as if I no longer existed. Those six excruciating minutes passed, and they did things to my body that I didn't even notice, some stitching and prodding, some assessing of the damage. The only voice that was directed toward me was that of the doctor between my legs, explaining the degree of tearing I had endured while she stitched me up.

(Third-degree tearing, I remember she told me, with an additional assurance that it *wouldn't be that bad.* I still think about finding her and telling her that it was that bad, that I didn't walk for a week, and that I wore adult diapers for more weeks than I'd like to count. I'd like to find her and tell her that on day two I was crumpled on the floor weeping and writhing from pain, that I urinated more than once in the upstairs hallway of my home because even with my husband's help, I couldn't make it thirty feet to the bathroom in time, that when I finally saw my family doctor for the state of my own health and not my baby's, she looked at me in horror and prescribed much better painkillers than the hospital had recommended I buy from the local pharmacy.)

That sudden influx of specialists who hovered over my daughter, who examined her tiny lungs for possible infection, who discerned whether or not she should be rushed even farther away from me, drifted in and out of our kindly lit hospital room like ghosts. Despite the intrusion of their bodies, when she was finally returned to me it was just the two of us, so much so that I barely remember that kind-faced doctor sewing up the tattered pieces of my shattered body while I stared into my daughter's face.

I laboured over three calendar days—twenty-seven hours where many things happened and nothing happened at all—but I was only given a room and bed in the hospital for two nights postpartum. The second night was a gift of timing: because my daughter was born after midnight, we got an extra day to sleep in proximity to immediate medical safety. That extension had nothing to do with the length and difficulty of the birth, nothing to do with the fact that my body had been torn and then stitched up, that my bladder wasn't yet functioning properly and was being monitored, that I couldn't walk unaided.

In the deepest part of that first night, I stared at my daughter's beautiful face for hours, barely aware of the nurses coming in intermittently to check her vitals and mine, to change the shoddy ziplocked ice pack between my legs, to give me over-the-counter Tylenol for my prescription-level wounds. I drank my room-temperature beef broth from the hospital tray, took my useless pills, and concerned myself with watching her sleep, each miraculous tiny exhale from her mouth proof that we had, in some otherworldly mystery, both made it to that dimly lit place together.

She was perfect and, despite everything, I was deliriously happy.

I had spent most of my adult life to that point only barely coping, grappling with various incarnations of clinical anxiety—hypochondria, agoraphobia, claustrophobia, and intrusive thoughts. I had experienced an irrational fear of disaster and dying, an ongoing flight impulse, and a penchant for panic attacks at the most inopportune times. I found being alone in the world difficult, yet I also found being surrounded by people difficult.

But here, with her, there was stasis. A pocket where it was only the two of us. A bridge we stood on together for a time, in no real hurry to get to the other side. There was no pain despite the very real pain, no fear despite the very real risk—just the sound of breath and quiet.

After so much loss, and waiting, and prayer, we had made it. Together.

In the dark of that room, in the middle of the night, I vaguely understood that something was now wrong with my body, something that would ultimately take weeks and then years to heal. But confined to that bed with her, still in the stained hospital gown I had been wearing since I arrived, the parts of me that had been sacrificed didn't matter. I remember quite clearly, in that calm moment on the sea of her birth, the freeing realization that *I didn't matter anymore*—a fact that would play out on multiple levels in the days, weeks, months, and even years to follow.

As a joke, my husband and I came to call her "the miracle child," the words whispered to each other in a comical caricature voice. But after so many years of infertility, after giving up, that's exactly what she was.

Many people—mostly men—have told me that after their children were born they were completely terrified to leave the hospital. When I was visibly pregnant, they would often give me a standard, unsolicited speech about how they couldn't believe they had been entrusted with the care and feeding of this precious, tiny, helpless, alien being. How on earth could the doctors just let them leave with this beautiful baby? How were they even allowed to go home? How would they even know what to do?

But by the second morning after her birth, I couldn't wait to get away from the hospital and its constant stream of what felt like trivial invasions. I couldn't wait until people finally stopped examining me, testing me, touching me, explaining to me, and instructing me. I couldn't wait to get my daughter home and into our bed where I intended to stay forever—*at least it was safe there*, I thought.

In the dark corners of that temporary room lurked all the anxieties I had forgotten when my body had purpose, when it was doing what it was supposed to.

Despite the fact that I couldn't walk on my own, my request for a wheelchair ride to the car was met with mild annoyance. The only genuine barrier to leaving the hospital was whether or not my husband could get my daughter securely into her detachable car seat, a task sternly observed and then approved of by a veteran nurse in our hospital room while my daughter slept snuggly in her much-too-big dinosaur pyjamas.

We were free to go.

I sat in the hospital lobby in that hard-won wheelchair, watching the seasonally abnormal February rain fall while waiting for my husband to pull the car out from the underground parking lot, holding tightly to my baby in the car seat in my lap and already sure something terrible was going to happen.

It's normal to be worried, they said.

What happens to a violated body when it gives birth? Is it reminded or is it transformed? Can it be both?

Despite the numerous professionals who assured me how normal everything was, there was nothing about the experience of my daughter's birth that felt that way. "Normal" is a hideous word, and one I have come to hate. The "normal" I experienced was a long period of very difficult time where I was more than sure I would never feel okay again. Where I was terrified that the damage after birth was irrevocable, and even more terrified by the fact that as a result I couldn't be the mother I wanted to be.

Twenty-seven hours of labour and four hours of pushing an overdue posterior baby. The word "tachycardia" spoken out loud. A word I vaguely recalled from the dozens of episodes of *Grey's Anatomy* I had watched while sprawled out on the couch during my third trimester, but in the moment couldn't for the life of me pull up the definition. The threat of a C-section when there wasn't progress. (It was me that wasn't progressing—it was always me.) Talk of suction and talk of forceps. The searing pain of Pitocin-stimulated delivery. The beeping monitors, the flashes of concern on attending faces, and the sheer strength of my fear pushing my daughter out of the peril of my difficult, unruly body.

(It was always the peril of my body.)

It was a traumatic birth. I can say that to myself now. But there were tender moments, and joyful moments, and even funny moments. I did keep watching *Jurassic World* in those first hours of labour. Our doula had recommended we decide on what she referred to as an "epidural safe word," something unrelated to birth that could be said out loud if I was entirely sure I wanted to see the anesthesiologist. As a result I was screaming baseball pitcher Marcus Stroman's name over and over again during the early morning drive to the hospital. Never before a John Fogerty fan, I did inexplicably request that Creedence Clearwater Revival be played in the delivery room after the epidural took effect at the seventeen-hour mark. ("Hope you got your things together, hope you are quite prepared to die," he wailed, and as a result of that memory, "Bad Moon Rising" is now referred to by my daughter as a "Mommy song.") When it finally came time to push, I was so overcome by nausea I projectile vomited directly in the face of the attending obstetrician. She had unfortunately forgotten to put her mask on. (Perhaps that last detail is really only funny in retrospect.)

In that room there were emotions beyond words. There was genuine strength and vulnerability and humour. There was a transcendent, near-animal acceptance of what needed to be done. There was fear, but a complete freedom from anxiety I hadn't felt in a very long time.

I was, indeed, quite prepared to die.

Maybe, within the systems we have created, all births are in part traumatic. The autonomy of the mother has been stolen under the directive of the doctor. Consent has been replaced with the convenience and urgency of simply moving things along. Robustness of care has been budgeted away, to the point where, after not eating for days, I ordered in my own meal beyond the broth and Jell-O they provided, and sent my husband out for the antacids and adult diapers I definitely needed. The necessity of recovery has been cut short by economy. The monumental transition has been disrupted by unrealistic expectations and painfully shoehorned into everyday life. No longer can we rest or lavish in the splendour of what we have created—instead we must bounce back quickly, not only with our "before and after" bodies but also with our work, our relationships, and our lives.

We cannot acknowledge this spectacular change, this spectacular transformation, but instead are forced to hide it from the world.

Experts who believe that pain is in your mind range from the spiritual to scientific kind, but they all seem to share a consensus that there is truth to the idea of mind over miserable matter. When you're grappling with genuine discomfort this feels like a flippant way to talk about the experience. It suggests discomfort is nothing more than an illusion, something conjured by a faulty, inexperienced, or undeveloped brain. That you're simply not made from tough enough stuff. Even worse, it infers that pain is simply made up, for attention or for care, or for no discernible reason at all.

I remember when I was a little girl and the accusation that pain was "made up"—or should be dealt with without complaint—first surfaced. At a second-grade basement sleepover, another child accidentally kneeled on my leg in the dark and popped out my kneecap momentarily. Instead of getting any medical attention, my screams were met with accusations of faking it, from the children and parents alike. Similarly, I remember in third-grade gym class when, thanks to an ill-advised (and incomplete) flip on a trampoline, that same knee collided with my face and caused a gusher of a nosebleed. I was then forced to sit through an afternoon of classes with tissues stuffed up my nose because it "wasn't a big deal."

Like most women of my generation, I was taught from a very early age that I was overreacting, that I was "being difficult," and that my pain—both emotional and physical—really needed to be bad enough to be worth complaining about. Who exactly gets to decide what is "bad enough" and what is "difficult" remains unclear, but the result was that I came to question my own mind, and my own experience of what felt intolerable.

My third trimester marked the start of various incarnations of pelvic discomfort (including a condition laughably nicknamed "lightning crotch"), but since my daughter's birth it has manifested as severe and persistent right-hip pain. I can manage without painkillers, but some days I limp along and have trouble sleeping. I see a chiropractor and various massage therapists. Sometimes I lie in rooms that have soft lighting with dreamy pan flute music playing; other times I receive more clinical, aggressive, even painful treatment. I tour a number of health care options until I finally land on a physiotherapist who specializes in pregnant and postpartum women.

I like my physiotherapist because she is forthright about my body being a puzzling project. She stares at it for long periods of time, telling me she very much enjoys these kinds of riddles, that they keep her up at night, trying to decipher exactly what went wrong to create this dull ache in my day-to-day. There has been no car accident, no dramatic sports injury, no real obvious source for my persistent agony. There is no explanation. My hip simply hurts, with no known cause. It's a mystery I am paying her to solve.

During each appointment she has a thoughtful and endearingly serious look on her face. She asks me to walk around, pace back and forth in her tiny office. She gets me to stand on one foot and then the other. She gets me to lie on my front, and my back, and then on each side. She makes a number of perplexed sighing noises. She manipulates me and generously provides temporary relief, pressing her fingers into sore spots and stretching out inexplicable tension. I'm grateful to her, even if she feels like she is failing me.

One day she explains exactly what professionals mean when they say that pain is in your mind.

"I hate telling clients that because it seems dismissive, as if their pain isn't real," she says. "But when the body is under threat the mind sends signals to be protective, to tense up, and that can cause enduring pain—even when the threat is long gone."

When she tells me this, I think about all the times my body has been under perceived threat. How it has retreated and surrendered. How it has fought.

When I talk about my daughter's birth, I am often dismissive of what happened during those twenty-seven hours. I am flip about the multiple people who reached deep inside me and twisted her tiny body clockwise until she was facing "the right way." When I remember that day, I feel somewhat outside myself, outside of the memory itself, as if another person lay there on the bed and endured the invasion. The gratitude that she was all right seemed to obliterate everything that happened to my body and all the indignities that would follow.

My physiotherapist thinks that there's something to that common feminist refrain that trauma lives in the body. She believes it would be a natural conclusion that the mind would seek to protect sites of former trauma, that it would tense up to the point of discomfort, even if there is no immediate threat. For this reason, the pelvis—where so many women have been invaded and violated—is a natural site of enduring pain. There are invasions that blindside us, and invasions we consent to, and invasions that are unclear, but the mind and the body can't differentiate—they all endure. These transgressions, regardless of intent, leave a lasting stain.

Trauma is not just a debilitating memory, but the cruel obliteration of our body's ability to cope with even the simplest of daily tasks.

I lie on my back, legs bent and knees pointing towards the ceiling. My physiotherapist pulls my thighs open, her hand on my right knee, and I involuntarily tense up, resist. My body doesn't trust her, even though my mind knows I am safe in her care. She tells me to work on it, but I'm not even sure what I am supposed to be working on. What is buried there—in both my body and my mind—that doesn't trust the hands of a professional hoping to heal me? What is my memory hiding to keep me safe?

Months pass postpartum and my curious physiotherapist mostly succeeds in alleviating my hip pain. I can walk down the street without discomfort, and thanks to her direction, I feel stronger and more capable.

But a dull nagging ache remains, one we can't get to the root of. One that I will never get to the root of. There are days when it disappears, where I all but forget it was ever there, only to have it return mockingly a few days later. Reminding me I will never be rid of it.

My trauma lingers like a whisper for years and years, reminding me to be ever alert.

"Stay vigilant," it says. "Never let the invasions happen again."

When my baby was only a few hours old, a nurse dropped me on the way to my first visit to the bathroom. My legs were still loose and uncertain post-epidural, and I landed face down on the floor—stunned, sore, and apologetic. As I pulled myself up, I just wanted to get back to the bed, back to my daughter.

My body had stubbornly refused to co-operate during delivery and now it was being punished. Instead of opening voluntarily like it was supposed to, it had to be torn and broken, like a branch violently separated from a tree during a storm.

For a long time after that I wouldn't be able to stand on my own, to walk unaided, to lift my baby out of her bassinet. When I did manage a few steps in the week that followed, I moaned in pain, stitched up and swollen, flesh torn and screaming red. Muscles had been ripped and otherwise obliterated, and simple body movements became impossible. I wasn't able to change my daughter's diaper or hold her while standing up. Breastfeeding was also a struggle—I couldn't sit upright for long enough without pain. For what felt like a very long time I could only manage to lie in bed, next to my baby, demoralized by my own incapacity.

Because of my difficulties breastfeeding, my daughter was losing weight, and even though I was exhausted by the very idea of another person touching my body, my husband convinced me to let him call a lactation consultant. I was desperate enough to let a stranger into our house during such a vulnerable time.

When the consultant appeared in our bedroom doorway, I remember my first thought was that she was beautiful. She had long strawberry-blonde hair parted down the middle and a warm, round, open face. She sat on the edge of our bed and I told her the dramatic plot points of my daughter's birth, now scanning that face for any look that would validate what I was feeling.

The doctors and nurses did such a good job, she's healthy, that's all that matters, I'm so grateful.

As I rattled off the details, I was really asking, "What counts as a difficult birth?"

I couldn't tell you her name, but as she sat next to me, I wept in her arms. She held me, knowing from experience that my already-clouded mind was full of the messy, unhelpful buzz of unsolicited advice and Googled expertise, of what I thought was supposed to happen versus what had actually happened.

And though I remember so little from that period—don't remember if I ate or slept or showered—I do remember something that strawberry-blonde lactation consultant said to me while I was crying in her arms, something that applied to the entire experience of having a child.

"You have to let go of everything you know," she said.

I understood then, in my shattered state, that my body had surrendered in a whole new way. It didn't betray me. It was willing to give up everything just to get this baby into the world, and that was powerful in itself.

I had bravely embraced my own irrelevance instead of having it dictated to me by someone else.

For years my body and life were defined almost entirely by trauma and fear. It was a story written by men and about what they did to me, a story I had to recite, in private and in public, over and over again in the hope of healing, in the hope of being heard or giving purpose to pain, often feeling worse off after I did. It's a story I shared only to feel further invaded. It was a story that made me, a story I had to tell in tiny windowless offices to professionals who promised a cure for my worry, my misery, my suffering. It was a story I had to prove, the only one that ever felt worth anything even though it left me feeling worthless.

"I got hurt, and then I got really sick, and then I mostly got better," I said. "I have a difficult past," was the story I told. It was one written in my skin, in my flesh, in my bone. It followed me everywhere I went, unrelenting, a script on repeat, a limp in my step.

And I don't have to tell it anymore.

My daughter changed my body's story. She taught me that my body was capable of doing something beyond what others wanted it to do, that it could exist in a place beyond suffering, beyond the seemingly endless recovery from that suffering, beyond *difficult*. My daughter taught me that my body existed for purposes higher than being used, or violated, or discarded, by myself or others. That it didn't need to simply be begrudgingly tolerated or mostly ignored.

My daughter taught me to live inside that body again, to be present and feel whole, even with all the physical pain her entrance into the world brought. She taught me to lean into discomfort in aid of working through and discarding it. She taught me that my body was more than troubled days and messy feelings, more than scars, more than stories told to prove something. More than admired frailty, fitting into someone else's spaces, and fears gathered up while weeping on the bathroom floor. More than a small bird beneath someone's open palm.

I may have been broken like a branch off a tree in a storm, but my daughter taught me how capable I truly was of regrowth.

A Normal Level of Worry

As soon as there is life there is danger.

—Germaine de Staël, often attributed to Ralph Waldo Emerson

The room where I used to write gets great light in the morning.

With a door that shuts and the understanding that you had to knock gently before entering, that room was a hallowed room of one's own. During a particularly productive period of my life, it was a place where I plotted novels and constructed essays and laboured through the minutia of copy edits. It was a place where I wrote about hundreds of baseball games and dozens of baseball players, transcribed my interviews with the likes of literary legend Joan Didion and *Law & Order* producer Dick Wolf, delivered winking takes on press screenings of *Magic Mike XXL* and *Sharknado 3*, and reviewed countless new releases from writers like Helen Humphreys, Margaret Atwood, and Heather O'Neill. It was a place where I delighted in those first generative moments of a manuscript, panicked over quick-turnaround newspaper and magazine deadlines, and worked deliriously on some half-formed idea deep into the night.

There was a certain messy charm in there—charming, of course, because the mess belonged to me. Box scores, poetry, and postcards were pinned to the bulletin board; movie posters hung on the wall; and multicoloured sticky notes reminded me of birthdays, appointments, and fleeting ideas. When the beautiful custom-made built-in shelves could no longer house the never-ending supply of books that came through our front door, piles accumulated along the walls, haphazard little towers beneath the very window that let in all that great morning light.

I only noticed that great morning light after it was no longer the room I wrote in.

Four months before my daughter was born, in a predictable frenzy of "nesting," my husband and I dismantled that home office and turned it into a spare bedroom. I lumbered around, hugely pregnant, filling bankers boxes with files, enthusiastically scrubbing dingy baseboards, and discarding old marked-up first and second drafts. Those magazines I wrote for were recycled and those teetering piles of books donated. Then the tiny space got the full benefit of my burgeoning (and frankly unhinged) maternal instinct and was transformed into a cozy place to host visitors.

We moved the queen-sized bed out of what was now designated the baby's room and rebuilt it where my desk used to be, making it up with a friendly navy-blue polka-dotted bedspread and a collection of matching throw pillows. Above the headboard we hung some artwork and a few floating shelves on which I styled an eclectic mix of my favourite books—Didion's *Play It as It Lays,* Chad Harbach's *The Art of Fielding,* Tony Burgess's *Pontypool.* The red painted side table got a handsome-looking lamp and a little white vase, a leftover centrepiece from our wedding a decade earlier. Once we were done the mammoth task, I popped a single deep-pink dahlia in the vase and took a picture.

"Feeling pretty damn proud of myself," I wrote when I showcased the newly styled room on social media.

It seemed logical to prioritize a welcoming guest room over a place for me to write. We were, after all, anticipating guests—people who would stay through the night and wake up early, who would help us with all the things we felt woefully unequipped to handle alone in those early days of new parenthood. The reorganization was fuelled by fantasies of someone taking the baby while I got some rest, or a shower. Besides, I could always write at our kitchen table. Help was surely more important than whatever work I thought I'd get done in those early days and weeks and months—a time that was, from what I had been consistently told, supposed to include some of the best moments of my life.

When I reflect on that eager transformation, it occurs to me that I never visualized exactly who those helpful people were going to be. I never thought about the identity of the magical visitors who would hold my baby while I ate a meal or changed out of my milk-stained pyjamas. These mysterious, generous souls remained abstract to me all the way up until the end, and then after that I was too afraid—too anxious—to actually ask for all the help I had so diligently made room for.

"Bask in those newborn snuggles," more experienced mothers with presumably lapsed memories told me in the final days of my pregnancy.

"It's such a special time," they said.

Those first days and weeks after my daughter's birth were shrouded in a fuzzy haze of chaos. As people generously left small congratulatory gifts on our doorstep and thoughtful cards in our mailbox, sent food and flowers and well wishes, I found those "best moments" very literally excruciating.

Post birth, with my stitches and inflatable donut pillow, I was intensely lonely and in a lot of pain. On my doula's wise advice, I was confined to the top floor of our home while my husband, who was able to take a few months of paternity leave, doted on me and our new baby. It was difficult to appreciate him properly under a grey cloud of unmedicated agony, difficult to connect with him when we were sleeping in shifts and barely able to talk about anything beyond what the baby did or didn't need.

And what the baby did or didn't need became my primary, obsessive preoccupation.

My exhausted—perhaps even hallucinating—mind would intrusively flash with all sorts of dire scenarios in which my new daughter would come to harm. Worry became the constant droning sound in the background of my days, intent on clouding the sweetness of our first precious moments together, sabotaging the blissful glow of new motherhood that had been promised to me by the Instagram posts of so many rosy beige-clad "momfluencers."

In the deep freeze of winter, largely immobile, I tried to stave off a host of imagined threats via the "support" of internet-fuelled paranoia. With my daughter's bassinet by my side and my smartphone in my hand, the accumulating list became vast.

Second-hand smoke was an obvious well-known no-no for baby, but a few stray articles proclaimed the new villain in the mix: "third-hand cigarette smoke," or residual nicotine and other chemicals left on surfaces like clothing or carpets. That meant anyone who was a smoker or came into brief contact with smokers would have to shower before stepping within a few feet of my child. More covertly hidden toxins were of course everywhere—scented candles, air fresheners, drugstore cosmetics—their poisons inhaled or absorbed though my skin and ominously lurking in my breast milk. A pillow, baby blanket, or gifted stuffed animal too close to my baby's face was apt to suffocate her. An improperly positioned baby carrier or poorly buckled car seat meant certain death.

In a hypochondria-by-proxy prison of my own making, I googled charts that statistically tracked the risk of SIDS (sudden infant death syndrome) week by week. When my daughter wasn't directly in my eyeline, I religiously stared at her on our black-and-white video monitor, the device diligently carried with me from room to room. Eventually I ended up making the absurd (and impossible) demand that either my husband or I had to be awake in the house at all times to keep watch while the baby was sleeping.

(And yes, I realize now how crazy this all sounds.)

Breastfeeding—something emphasized as vital by every pamphlet I was handed, every book I read, and every class I took—was a struggle. In our early days my daughter wasn't gaining weight optimally and I punished myself for that "failure," taking it on as yet another thing to compulsively worry about. The meticulous feeding records I kept in the notes section of my phone now horrify me to even look at. Each day I would track when and how much my daughter was fed, whether it was from the breast or pumped into a bottle, trying to ensure she was getting enough nourishment with no genuine way of really knowing. These notations ooze with helpless desperation, are heavy with both intense fear and punishing monotony.

Despite the urging of people who cared about me ("Fed is best!" those more experienced mothers would exclaim when I lamented my meagre milk production), I flat-out refused to use formula.

"We can supplement," my exhausted husband begged. "It's okay if it's what's best for her—what's best for you. And it might mean you could get some sleep?"

I remember looking at him like he was insane, remember shaking my head dramatically and refusing his perfectly logical suggestion. *Breastfed babies have lower risk of asthma and diabetes,* I thought. *Breastfed babies are less likely to have ear infections and stomach issues. Breastfed babies are less likely to die suddenly without explanation.*

I hadn't slept more than a few hours at a time, hadn't changed out of my jogging pants or washed my face with more than a makeup wipe, hadn't done much more than salve my chapped nipples and eat all the lactation cookies my husband had diligently baked.

"I don't want her to have formula," I insisted, immediately going back to obsessing about how best to get my daughter's weight up.

Of course I should have given her formula, of course fed is always best, but my husband's desperate pleading was no match for the combination of my anxiety disorder and all those months of consistent breastfeeding indoctrination. My sunk cost rationale was that I'd come too far to simply give up on getting breastfeeding "right." Instead, I insisted we opt for the complicated and doctor-recommended process of "finger-feeding," a method that involved pumping copious amounts of breastmilk and then pushing it through a tiny tube taped to either my finger or my husband's.

During those frenzied, worry-ladened days, time itself became meaningless. The only fixed points were appointments with doctors (to track the weight my daughter wasn't gaining) or our lactation consultant (to help my daughter gain weight) or pelvic floor physiotherapists (to improve my battered body so I could sit properly and better help my daughter gain weight).

Because I had experienced significant physical trauma via pregnancy, labour, and birth, my pelvic floor was, to put it mildly, a mess. My bladder was recovering but generally uncooperative. Because of this I voluntarily suffered the indignity of internal physio exams and therapeutic treatments that wouldn't even gift me the anonymity of clinical distance. Instead, an upbeat, warm woman cheerily chatted with her fingers deep inside me, the sound of ocean waves lapping in the background (something I assume was supposed to be soothing). I would dutifully try to conceal the pain as I was adjusted and prodded accordingly, a professional looking for evidence I was healing properly while pushing out a conciliatory "you look so great."

At one of my more invasive pelvic floor appointments, my baby became inconsolably hungry in the waiting room. My husband had to bring her to me during the examination, which meant my internal exam was completed with her on my breast and my husband by my side. It seemed I wasn't even allowed to be humiliated alone.

Beyond attending a litany of appointments for both my daughter and me, the only things to do were to pump and feed and soak my healing body in Epsom salt baths. During those lonely early days, the television in the bedroom was on constantly, and I watched entire seasons of prime-time comedy shows, and procedural cop shows, and heart-tugging dramas. I watched cooking shows, and stand-up comedy, and the LA Dodgers or the San Francisco Giants play their west-coast games deep into the night. I staved off whatever hypothetical disaster was currently haunting my brain by keeping a careful, TV-aided vigil next to my daughter's bassinet (of course the one that came highest recommended for staving off SIDS), both of us bathed in the blue light of an infinite flickering screen.

In rare moments of sleep, I would have nightmares that my daughter was lost and I was trying desperately to find her, grasping in the darkness with a deep sense of hopelessness. It seemed like there was something poisonous lurking inside my head, a voice that warned if I looked away for even a moment she would disappear, evaporate into the air, as if she was something I had dreamed up after years of lack, something that could be snatched away from me at any moment.

Outings immediately postpartum were understandably rare. February in Toronto wasn't exactly ideal for going for a walk with a newborn, and it took weeks for my stitches to dissolve, my wounds to sufficiently heal, and for me to trust that my battered, leaky bladder wouldn't betray me at an inopportune moment. When we did venture out beyond those mandatory doctor's appointments, it was always for supplies and always within a few blocks of our house—to the local coffee shop, grocery store, pharmacy, or medical supply store.

About a month after my daughter's birth, I was feeling adventurous and suggested we wander to a nearby brewery, an excursion that demanded a relatively low investment but had the potential to make me feel somewhat human again. I replaced my standard jogging pants with a pair of elasticized jeans and pulled on an oversized red maternity sweater, strapping my tiny daughter into her newly minted baby carrier. (I'd been spending a not insignificant amount of time practising getting her in and out of it, watching instructional YouTube videos and heeding the warnings that she be positioned correctly lest she suffocate against my chest.)

Pumped breast milk in the diaper bag meant I could enjoy a small beer, but I was ready to set a timer regardless, tracking exactly when it would be completely, totally, and utterly safe for her to feed again. (Another thing to track in the already long list of things to track.) The walk was less than ten minutes, but when the three of us arrived and settled onto a few bar stools I felt a significant sense of victory, like we were moving into a new phase that didn't involve near-constant convalescence, an inability to discern time of day, and that stupid inflatable pillow. Like there was a "normal" in our future, however different that might look from the normal of the past.

But as we sat there, sharing a flight of beer, I noticed a wall-mounted heater buzzing away high above our heads, its orange glow working hard against the sub-zero weather outside the industrial brewery's closed garage door. My face flushed and sweat began to accumulate under my heavy cardigan, my daughter pressed tightly against me, peaceful, lightly snoring.

Acute exposure to ambient heat may be a risk factor for SIDS mortality, the National Library of Medicine website had told me during one of my late-night Google deep dives. *Being too warm while sleeping can increase a baby's risk of SIDS*, the Mayo Clinic website had warned via the glow of my phone's screen.

Surely the experts weren't being irrational? Surely the threat was real?

A mere twenty minutes after arriving, I looked down at my sleeping baby and demanded we leave because the room felt "too hot." I knew my husband was reluctant, but he acquiesced and paid the bill. By then it was impossible to argue with my worries, too exhausting to dismantle them. I'd spent so much time (and done so much research) building them up.

The wall heater buzzed and burned away threateningly as we abandoned our half-empty drinks and headed home.

For years my life had been defined by wanting a baby. Surely I could be allowed to finally have one? Surely I wouldn't tempt fate by enjoying a beer and the moment? Surely I could become a mother without being unimpeachably diligent and constantly terrified?

It was terror that, to many, likely seemed crazy. But to me, holding a baby I never thought I would be able to have, it felt entirely necessary. Control had long been the way I mitigated my anxiety. Now it was my personal vise grip, squeezing everything and everyone I loved into manageable submission.

Postpartum anxiety (PPA), defined simply as "excessive worrying" that occurs after having a baby, is postpartum depression's (PPD) less-discussed sibling, yet they often arrive together.

"Postpartum anxiety syndromes have recently been gaining more academic and clinical attention and are now understood to be a significant part of PPD," Karen R. Kleiman and Valerie Davis Raskin explain in their book *This Isn't What I Expected*. "Panic disorder and obsessive-compulsive disorder are present at a rate of about 2 percent each in the general population, and both may be first diagnosed after, or exacerbated by birth."

Much like PPD, PPA tends to be connected to hormonal changes in the postpartum period, and as Harvard Health Publishing editorial advisory board member Stephanie Collie writes, "mothers experiencing postpartum depression commonly experience symptoms of anxiety, although not all mothers suffering from anxiety are depressed."

All through my pregnancy, medical professionals, brochures, and online articles repeatedly cautioned me to look for evidence of postpartum depression, something beyond the simple baby blues—a sadness that wouldn't abate, crying that wouldn't stop—but I don't remember anyone mentioning how common postpartum anxiety was. A few weeks post birth I received a follow-up call from a public health nurse, asking me how I was feeling and screening me for those telltale signs of sadness. She somehow missed the grim frenzy of my dire thoughts completely.

"I'm doing great," I told her. She was glad.

I wasn't depressed, but I was certainly a prime candidate for "excessive worrying"—a history of mental health disorders, abuse, and trauma are all risk factors. And yet no one, from my initial pregnancy test to the postpartum period—not my family doctor, my obstetrician, or anyone at the hospital—had even broached the topic of my long relationship with anxiety, or the possibly of it bleeding into my day-to-day life as a mother.

"It is common for a woman with a history of anxiety to experience a worsening of these symptoms during the postpartum period," Kleiman and Raskin write. "Most women with PPD have severe anxiety symptoms, including worrying, ruminating, panic attacks, and agitation. Anxiety attacks may be secondary to PPD or may be the primary problem."

Looking back, there was a sort of inevitability to the ease with which I quickly fell into the role of ridiculed and overwhelmed caricature—the hand-wringing mother who rarely took her baby out, who irrationally panicked in public spaces, who bathed everyone and everything in hand sanitizer, who heeded every warning however obscure, who banned bizarre things from the household, who woke every hour on the hour to lightly press a hand to her baby's chest to make sure it rose and fell. In the chaos of postpartum, the guardrails fell off. All the work I'd done in the past to keep my everyday worry at bay was obliterated by this monumental life shift and I suddenly felt completely useless.

In Jessamine Chan's heartbreaking dystopian novel *The School for Good Mothers*, a bad decision leads to Frida's young daughter being taken from her and subsequent training to become a "good mother." Via Frida's reflections on the struggle (and terror) of early parenting, Chan articulates that pervasive feeling of being wholly unequipped: "Each day, she searched Harriet's face for signs that death was imminent. There must be people who thrive under pressure, but not Frida. Maybe she shouldn't be trusted with any kind of life. Maybe people should have to work up to children, from plants to pets to babies. Maybe they should all be given a five-year-old, then four, then three, then two, then one, and if the child is still alive at year's end, then they can have a baby. Why did they have to begin with a baby?"

I used to feel capable, in my work, in my day-to-day, and now I was in charge of this world I knew nothing about. My old life was over but I felt totally alienated from my new one. Everyone else seemed to know exactly what they were doing, while I was a fraud, an imposter, a fake. I worried the baby knew it. I worried the baby was disappointed with what it got. I was disappointed with what the baby got.

Pregnancy made me feel powerful, fearless, and determined. Postpartum, it was as if every errant anxiety I had ever had in my entire life rose from dormancy and happily found a renewed sense of purpose. I have since heard that this is common among mothers who have experienced infertility and pregnancy loss. We have spent so much of our time wanting, hoping, and grieving that when our child does finally arrive it can feel impossible to get comfortable and enjoy it like we're "supposed to."

How can you "relax" and truly embrace something you fear will be taken from you—something that has been taken from you before?

I also found that in the wake of infertility it became very difficult to express any of the real physical, emotional, and mental health concerns that came with early motherhood. Whether your "infertility journey" was short or long, whether or not there was medical intervention, it's easy to feel as though the fact that you were able to have a baby at all should outweigh any loss of identity, frustration, or yearning for what came before, and of course severe anxiety or depression. Hide those feelings away. Shelve your worries and complaints and instead showcase your gratitude.

"A heartfelt thank you to everyone who sent warm thoughts, cheerful flowers, and delicious food to get us through some challenging moments," I wrote on social media on the day my daughter turned one month old. "Mom is definitely on the mend, and we're making our way into the world."

Was I definitely on the mend? Were we making our way into the world?

Before my daughter arrived, I had been one of *those women*—struggling, unmentionably barren, uncomfortable to be around, awkward to invite to baby showers. Then I got my baby—my narrative climax—obliterating the worry and struggle and pain that came before. My tragedy ended. But somewhere between the many appointments, diaper changes, pumping sessions, and sleep vigils, what infertility had done to me and my mental health still needed to be addressed. The grief endured because that story had also been my identity for so long—the story I told myself about myself. The wanting and waiting remained long after her first day in the world, and well into the years that followed.

I told everyone I was doing great, that motherhood came naturally to me, that I didn't feel like I was failing at every turn. I told everyone I was doing great because they were so happy for me, and because that was what they expected—what I expected—what had been depicted in every soft-focus glowing tableau of early motherhood I had ever seen, scenes I had been ravenously jealous of for so very long. I found myself saying out loud, over and over again, "But you know, I am just so thankful," no matter the sadness or sickness or brokenness or loneliness or terror I was feeling at the time. No matter how torn up or defeated or tired I was. No matter how deeply I came to yearn even an hour of quiet, a reprieve from my buzzing electrical storm of a brain.

I had a baby now. I got not only what I signed up for but also what I begged, worked, and prayed for, for years. I paid for that privilege in torn tissue and loose ligaments and body fatigue and hormonal misery and a kind of sleeplessness akin to militaristic torture. I had paid for what I wanted most in the world via the dismissal of who I was and who I had hoped I would be one day. I had paid so much that on some days I felt like there was nothing left of me.

But instead of asking for help, I said that I was thankful. Over, and over, and over again.

Those imaginary people who were going to help us during the newborn haze never came to stay in our freshly scrubbed guest room. No one came over, held my hand, and offered instructions on all these things I was supposed to have already mastered.

The lack of help was the result of many factors. I have older parents, and because I am an only child with no siblings I grew up with, there was no one around to play the role of aunt or uncle. Most of my extended family lives overseas. At the time my daughter was born, many of my close friends were childfree and likely didn't even understand what kind of help I would need. (Certainly not something I can fault them for given that I didn't even understand the help I would need.) But, looking back, I think the primary reason for the lack was something deeper. When I later complained to a close friend about that near-total absence of an extra set of hands, she gently pointed out that my multi-faceted anxiety wouldn't have let anyone in the door anyway.

I was anxious because I didn't have help, but I didn't have help because I was too anxious to invite it in.

Not long after my daughter was born, I read a magazine article about a woman who confessed to thinking about her baby in a large pot of boiling water. She said that as soon as that image found its way into her mind, she knew she had to seek help immediately. I remember thinking how brave she was to say that ugly all-consuming thing out loud, to face the very real worry that people would think she actually wanted to harm her child, when, really, she was just so terrified of potential harm that it consumed her every thought, every day.

I had so much empathy for this woman, this stranger, and yet it never occurred to me that my thoughts and feelings could be connected to any sort of postpartum disorder. Surely all new mothers were worried as much as I was about all this impending doom? Surely they were consumed by every safety warning label and research study and ill-placed piece of advice? Surely they checked and rechecked safety buckles and door locks repeatedly, read ingredient lists religiously, googled everything and then googled it all over again? Surely they were paralyzed by a daily fear of germs and unleashed dogs and playground injuries, by the knowledge that their hearts were now beating outside their bodies, out in the world with a million potential threats?

I never told anyone about my anxious feelings. Of course, the people closest to me suspected I was struggling with more than my physical woes, thought the rules I set up around keeping the baby safe were bizarre at best, but I never reached out or begged for a break. I never consulted any of those pamphlets I had been given for numbers to call or websites to visit because I wasn't actually "sad."

It's normal to be worried, they said.

I'm doing great, I said.

There is this commonly tossed around (and frankly lazy) rhetoric when it comes to having kids, this idea that you have "never really known love" until you have brought a child into your life. It's an assertion that had always annoyed me, and that then made me furious when I was grappling with infertility: insult added to injury that I would never truly understand what it meant to love if I remained childless.

After having my daughter, I realized that it's not so much that you have never known love—it is that you have not yet known this kind of extreme capacity for loss. A baby comes into your life and the daily potential for devastation clings to you, squirms in your lap, demands you attend to it. It fills all the corners of your days and leaves you on high alert. What I do remember from those early days, more than anything else, is being overwhelmed by how dangerous this kind of love can be, suddenly understanding not only that it could provoke the greatest grief but also that it could easily make me abandon my entire sense of self.

You would think that, when this very real fear of loss affects so many mothers, we wouldn't mock and deride and ignore motherly worry the way we do, wouldn't punish or pathologize it, and certainly wouldn't be so callous as to label a worried mother a "problem." Instead, the cartoonish overbearing mother has become both a comedic and horrific pop culture staple—she's tightly wound; wringing her hands; unable to relax, let go, and simply take pleasure in the joys of motherhood. She's Brian De

Palma's darkly comical depiction of Stephen King's Margaret White, fretting and forbidding Carrie to go to the prom ("They're all going to laugh at you"), or Nina Sayers's unnervingly involved mother obsessing over her daughter's fingernails in Darren Aronofsky's anxiety-ridden *Black Swan* ("It's all this pressure. I knew it would be too much. I knew it.").

The worried mother hovers. She fusses over her charges and inevitably fucks them up. She's laughed at, she's awkward, she's easily dismissed, she needs to calm down. At best she produces emotionally stunted snivelling nerds and at worst kitchen-knife-wielding serial killers with a penchant for shower scenes.

"Instincts vs. irrationality. Worry vs. care. Anxious vs. happy. Overprotective vs. rejecting. Realistic vs. dominant-culture sanctioned," writes Yael Goldstein-Love in her 2023 *Slate* essay "In Defense of the Anxious Mother." "Even if we consciously reject every one of these dichotomies as reductive, it's hard not to take them in and judge ourselves against them. And once we subject ourselves to their terms, we've doomed ourselves to failure."

Maybe it's because infertility and pregnancy loss have been pushed into very private places of suffering, but when a new mother reveals her perfectly natural and perhaps—given her experience of lack and loss—inevitable worry, she is at best lightly mocked and at worst told she is doing genuine harm. I can't tell you how many times I have been sternly warned by parenting manuals and experts that if I didn't rein in my anxiety, it would rub off on my infant, my toddler, my child.

"Keep these vulnerable little beings safe while also knowing you can't," Goldstein-Love continues. "And, whatever you feel in the face of this impossible task, make sure it's in no way affecting your behavior, except in exactly the moments and ways when it had better be."

I once privately confided in another mother about all those early, frantic, looping worries, shared my deep sense of shame about the places my mind would go when I didn't want it to. As someone who had experienced pregnancy loss, she understood where the storm came from, had empathy like I did for the woman with the boiling pot of water, and offered comfort in the form of commiseration.

"It's like 'oh what's the worst that could happen?' and then the worst—at least in terms of pregnancy—does happen. You miscarry. You lose your baby. And then you're like 'oh shit, well, I guess everything is fair game now.'"

Sometimes I wonder what terrible thing must befall a woman—a mother—to make her worry in those early days justified and tended to? How bad must it be for our culture to deem her level of concern and fear an understandable part of her experience, instead of just a detestable character trait that she'll pass along to her baby like a virus? When will we offer her the kind of reassurance, resources, help, and healing she needs, instead of warnings, derision, and, finally, judgment?

Now, years later, I am amazed I got through it all with that empty guest room—without extra hands beyond my entirely beleaguered husband's. But I have since come to learn that motherhood is just instance after instance of being amazed, over and over again—amazed by tiny fingers and toes; by bright blue eyes that settle into green; by the terrifying intensity of your love, your exhaustion, and your worry; by your own inexplicable fortitude.

"Enjoy all of it, it goes so fast."

A woman says this to me in the checkout line at the grocery store, smiling toward my daughter—my miracle child. Old enough to be strapped in the cart, she is clutching a bottle of sriracha and babbling nonsensically.

I nod and smile, but know the truth is it doesn't actually go fast.

Yes, I think back on those frenzied newborn days and wonder where the time went, what I was doing, and how I was feeling, but I never forget that those days were actually excruciatingly long. I remember that I lost myself in the relentless looping worry and the lack of momentum, consumed by the solitary goal of her survival to the point of madness. Time can feel so goddamn slow while you're so deep in it, when you're anxious, when you're recovering, when you feel like you've drifted so far away from who you actually are.

Every morning there were ominous oceans of time to fill, and in those waves, I seemed to flounder haplessly, performing tasks I felt unequipped to perform. Feed the baby, change the baby, make sure the baby gets down for her nap. How much tummy time is the right amount of tummy time? What is the safest way to sleep to avoid the worst kind of tragedy? Something as simple as getting the stroller out the front door and down the front steps felt impossible when compounded by dozens of other tiny items on the agenda, the dozens of other tiny questions that needed to be asked, the dozens of fears bouncing around my brain.

As my daughter got older and more robust, my worry thankfully faded. But it never entirely left me. Every time she runs a little too far ahead or loosens her grip on my hand crossing a busy street or disappears from view for a moment, I feel that familiar rise of panic and am forced to tamp it down. I still look at her beautiful face and see my heart beating outside of my chest, still vividly recall that I spent a majority of those early days staring at this exquisite life I'd created, racked with worry, praying that I could manage to keep said life aflame.

It goes so fast until it doesn't.

So many years later, reflecting on that early time and its terrifying absurdity, my heart breaks for my former self, a person consumed by pain, discomfort, and sheer terror—so much so that she couldn't enjoy those early moments that took forever to get to and through, but were gone so quickly.

Just before my daughter's first birthday, one of our two geriatric cats needed intense, entirely grotesque emergency abscess surgery. She returned from the vet with her back half shaved and, out of necessity, her wounds left open to heal properly. My former office, that guest room that visitors never slept in, became solely hers, one of our many baby gates affixed to the door to keep her safe from the cruelty of our second cat, the annoyance of our dog, and eventually the grabby fingers of our growing toddler.

My former office still housed my beautiful inherited rolltop desk, the place where I had written my last book. The idea of ever writing a book again felt impossible. The desk's dark wood surface had been overtaken by dust and stacks of stray papers, various books and magazines, and unopened mail, its cover ultimately closed permanently to hide the disarray.

The cat flourished in her own space long after her wounds healed. Her grey-and-white coat became glossy and thick again, her once hilariously grumpy disposition transforming into surprising warmth and affection. It seemed both humane and convenient to just give her the room permanently. (It would seem that rescued animals were often getting their own bedrooms in my home.) She wanted nothing more in the world than to be alone in comfort, so I left the once-temporary baby gate on the door to keep the other animals out and maintain her sanctuary. For hours at a time, she slept peacefully in a patch of light on the black upholstered office chair, coating it in a thick layer of fur, blissfully snoring while no person or animal bothered her.

She was, of course, very pleased.

Other Mothers

Who is she? That is the question I was starting to ask in all my books. Not who am I, though that comes into it. How does she get along in a world that has voided her?

—Deborah Levy, *The Position of Spoons*

The child I had waited so long for arrived the same week pitchers and catchers reported to major league baseball spring training in Florida and Arizona. This was a narrative detail so perfect I couldn't have invented it—a personally beloved time of rebirth coinciding with, well, literal birth.

For five years before my daughter's arrival, I had been down south with the ballplayers every preseason. At first I was there as an eager fan in the stands, drinking summer shandies and hollering my elation in the direction of the field. Then I was there as an earnest new sportswriter, proud of the shiny laminated lanyard proclaiming my access as I shoved my tape recorder in athletes' faces. While it made perfect sense that my daughter would make her debut during my favourite time of year, her arrival also carried with it another meaning I wouldn't decipher until later.

Even into my largely immobile third trimester, I fantasized about strapping a tiny person into a carrier on my body and taking in a baseball game, notebook in hand, ready to file a thoughtful piece on a newly acquired rookie. My daughter sleeping adorably while I interviewed players and wrote stories about their wins, losses, and the fact that they were in the best shape of their life.

I wouldn't forget myself like all those other mothers—I'd just reconfigure my life to make the new fit with the old.

"She's so calm," they would all coo. "What a good baby she is."

A few months before my due date, a fellow female sportswriter, one I admire greatly, told me that it took her seven whole years to find her footing again in the working world after her son was born.

"It took me a long time to come back to myself," she said. "But when I eventually did, I was better and even more myself than before."

I smiled and nodded and was horrified by her admission. *Seven years.* I promised myself it wouldn't happen to me. At the time I assumed the loss of identity, the general forgetting (and being forgotten) that comes with motherhood only happens to the weak and unfocused, those lacking passion and drive, their lives empty and waiting to be filled with play mats and playdates.

I, of course, was *different*—I loved my career and had fought relentlessly for it. I had put up with too much in the sexist worlds of literature and journalism and sports to simply give up and fade away into a cloth vs. disposable diaper debate. I had too fertile a mind to become preoccupied with whether or not my daughter was sizing out of her leggings, and whether or not her socks were no-slip. I would certainly never find myself fighting over a spot on a library play mat, or calling other women "mama," or in lieu of sleep watching my baby's tiny chest rise and fall throughout the night. I would make it all work and make it look effortless.

I wouldn't be like those *other mothers*, right?

I'm now embarrassed to confess that before I had a baby, I had done my fair share of quiet mockery of mothers' groups, mommy bloggers, and momtrepreneurs. I fell victim to the "us and them" divide that seeks to pit those with kids against those without them, that insists we squabble amongst ourselves instead of helping each other out, that prevents us from criticizing and dismantling the structures that are limiting and failing us all.

As a young working woman without any real access to the experience of childrearing, I wrongly assumed mothers' lives were easy, *luxurious* even—I mean, what did they have to complain about? When I worked an office job, I had watched from my cluttered desk as they got "so much time off" for maternity leave or got to go home early from work because of daycare or school pickups, not understanding the immense load they carried when they got off one clock just to get on another. I used to hate the way mothers seemed to take up so much space on sidewalks and in restaurants, the way they disturbed my meals and made a mess by proxy, never recognizing the lack of freedom and support they struggled through daily.

I assumed that the mothers who faded from view after the "welcome to the world" birth pic on Instagram had Neanderthal husbands in need of housewives to care for them. I had a progressive partner who supported my goals. I'd never need to family-meal or toddler-outfit plan. I would never schedule a baby music class over an in-studio radio spot, or prioritize nap time over a deadline. I would never choose my child at the expense of my career, never sacrifice my dreams to stay at home.

(For the record, I eventually did all those things.)

I am now deeply ashamed of what I assumed about mothers before I became one. That I believed the mother who shelved parts of her old life for a new one was "a failure," that she'd let herself be annexed, usurped, overtaken. That she had no drive, or that she didn't truly care about herself, or she didn't work hard enough.

How ridiculous that I assured myself I would never be "like that." That I'd simply be the same person I was, only with a baby. That I assumed all those things I'd thoughtlessly chided others about wouldn't happen to me.

Though I desperately wanted to become a mother—a feeling only made more desperate by the years I was unable to become one—I don't recall ever seeing any images of motherhood that resonated with me, only ones that didn't. I wasn't an angelic, nurturing goddess mama-type, dressed in gauzy pastels and making my own baby food from scratch. I wasn't that barrier-busting girlboss so prevalent in the mid-2010s, teetering on her jewel-tone stilettos while giving a TED Talk about the benefits of feminine energy in the workplace. I just wanted to be a great mom and maintain the work I loved, maintain the fragile sense of self that I had long cultivated—but the path to achieving that desire remained fuzzy no matter how many examples of modern motherhood the algorithm pushed into my feed.

The difficulty of my daughter's birth and my subsequent recovery banished any hope of a flourishing career with my newborn in tow. (Although I'm not sure an easier birth and recovery would have made any difference.) I wouldn't be going to Florida for spring training. I wouldn't be boarding a plane, taking in those beautiful southern ballparks, or reporting on the game I loved. I wouldn't be writing about baseball, or much of anything, for a very long time. As a result of that drought, I would find it very difficult to claw my way back to the page at all when the time came.

The long dream that was my daughter finally materialized, and I found I couldn't hold on to all the other dreams that I had propped up in her place.

At the local library baby story time, a bizarre hierarchy erupts.

The alpha moms always sit in the front, closest to the eternally smiling, ukulele-playing librarian. It doesn't actually matter what time they arrive, the space is always clear for them. They are making sure their babies get the best view of the picture books, the most interaction, the maximum emotional and intellectual benefit, because their babies are the *most important*.

There is a buzzing energy of self-assurance that comes off of the alpha moms, a confidence I myself don't have, but also one I know is actually a carefully constructed lie. Despite the fact that the alphas are perfectly put together in their hundred-dollar leggings and deliberately messy buns, I'm pretty confident they are faking it just like everybody else here is. Most of us first-time moms are all functioning with varying degrees of insecurity and terror—some are just better at hiding it (or care more about hiding it) than others.

Then there are the beta moms. They hang back a bit, chatting amongst themselves in quiet, kindly, reassuring tones. They are deeply sweet to each other insomuch as strangers can be deeply sweet, in a way that is both performative and appreciated. They are the "go easy on yourself" types, willing to admit how hard things can be and how unnecessary it is to be perfect every day. They are body positive, and "bad mom" positive, and pay earnest stock compliments, lightly offering tips and advice in a way that doesn't send the recipient into a full-body shudder of insecurity. They repost a lot of inspirational quotes on social media and use the word "mama" to refer to each other. They do yoga but are not very good at it.

Behind the sweet, kindly betas are "the caregivers," usually seated on chairs away from the play mat where all the important "baby socialization" takes place. When I first started coming to library story time I would always sit with them in the back, with my daughter on my lap, a function of my usual impulse to simply fade into the background, but I also appreciated basking in their non-judgmental knowledge. No one in this room is more relaxed, more secure in their ability than the back row of self-assured babysitters, nannies, and grandmas.

To be honest, I am mostly terrified here, which is hilarious but also painfully true. No television or radio spot, no celebrity interview or big game recap written on a deadline has properly prepared me for this performance. I don't even really like coming, but library story times are one of those things that suddenly become necessary when you have a baby. (Sign language classes! Swimming classes! Community drop-ins!) It is in spaces like this, spaces occupied by an overwhelming number of other mothers, that I most feel like I have no idea what I'm doing. Every movement feels excruciatingly forced. I sing songs and the words catch in my throat. I clap and wave my hands and feel the absurdity of my gestures.

Basically, I feel pretty damn stupid.

When my daughter was about ten months old, I reluctantly signed up for a Tuesday morning "baby and me" music class. The whole idea of it seemed kind of silly, but that overriding need to be a great mother prodded me to reserve a spot. Ubiquitous studies touted the benefits of music for babies, and my maternity leave–related loneliness suggested some scheduled social time, however out of character, might do me some good.

The music class was in a yoga studio above a coffee shop just down the street from our house, but every time I made the ten-minute trek it felt like a monumental achievement. With a mountain of baby-related necessities strapped to my back and my daughter strapped to my front, I would find a seat by the café window for fifteen minutes before it started, clutching my mug and marvelling that I had managed to get there at all.

When it was time for the mothers to gather (and it was always mothers), we would slip upstairs, peel ourselves out of our many winter layers, and find a spot in the circle, smiling awkwardly but kindly at each other. A young, beautiful woman with impossibly shiny long black hair and a guitar would sing inane children's songs in an overly sweet high-pitched voice. The other mothers and I would clap our hands at the right spots, make goofy faces to make our babies laugh, feeling lightly humiliated but altogether enamoured. We were all doing our best. We were all exhausted. But we had made it here together and were enjoying each other's company, helping each other, when the people we had hoped would help us "didn't want to be a bother."

One particular Tuesday morning there was a snowstorm. While I debated staying home, I knew there was some deeper meaning to me being able to suit us both up and get us the four blocks to the yoga studio with the beautiful songstress and my new crew of overtired moms. I always had something to prove in those early months, maybe because I felt like I was flailing and fumbling my way through this new life. Even the brief company of other people who were also flailing and fumbling was an unexpected salve. I clipped my daughter into her baby carrier and zipped her inside my coat, her smiling eyes peering up at me from beneath her big furry hat.

"We can do this—right, monkey?"

And we did. Four blocks in knee-deep snow and a brisk wind, to find our place in that sacred song circle, to sing about elephants and peanut butter sandwiches, to wipe noses and share knowledge and change diapers on the floor of the yoga studio's tiny bathroom. After everything I had achieved in my old life, it was amazing what I was now proud of, where I found comfort, the things that brought me satisfaction—meaningless, mundane, mine.

When the thirty-minute class was over we packed up, my baby and me a bundled team facing the storm. I didn't have much time to get home before she inevitably nodded off, and it was so important to get her in the crib before that happened. The hard-won crib nap was a small patch of time that belonged to me.

The wind whipped as I picked up my pace, her eyes heavy as we approached home.

"Stay awake, monkey," I singsonged to her, strapped to my front. "Just a few more minutes," I cooed, longing for that time alone, groping for my keys in my pocket.

And then, on our front walkway, I slipped.

I must have hit a patch of ice I couldn't see under the deep snow. I began to fall, face forward. Instinctively, to not flatten my daughter beneath my weight, I managed to twist and land on my side. I heard her small skull connect with the sheet of ice beneath the powder with a tiny clunk, heard her scream erupt like lava.

I got up immediately, pulled the furry hat from her head, and looked into her eyes. Her face was crimson with pain and fear, her soft head dotted with snow.

"It's okay, sweet girl," I repeated over and over, panicked, sweating, hot with anxiety.

In that panic I had dropped my keys. I had to get her inside. *Where were my keys?*

I was on my knees then, groping through the field of white with frozen, mitten-less hands, fingers burning, trying desperately not to tip too far forward and dip my screaming, injured baby in the snow. She didn't relent, her tiny wrinkled face shiny with tears, her volume at a fever pitch, audible over the whipping wind.

I finally found them, walked cautiously to the door, and got us both inside. After peeling off our many layers, I sat down with her on the living room couch to inspect where I was sure her skull had cracked open on the ice. She was intact, but so flushed, so frantic, and it was impossible to find the point of contact. When she was finally calm, her tense body relaxing on my shoulder, panic rose in me again—should I let her sleep or keep her awake? After some frantic googling I decided to lay her down in her crib, and for the full nap watched her tiny chest rise and fall. Forty-five minutes without ever lifting my eyes from her.

Our pediatrician saw my daughter at the first available appointment and was entirely unfazed. We were crammed into her closet of an examination room, the nurse practitioner blowing bubbles into the air, my daughter giggling, the doctor shining a small light in my daughter's eyes. A tiny blue-black bruise had begun to form on her forehead, a mark of shame I carried with me until it finally faded.

"Did she scream when she hit the ice?" the doctor asked, while (quite unbelievably, I thought) smiling.

I nodded meekly.

"That's a great sign. It means she didn't black out."

I am a good mother because she didn't black out. I am a good mother. I am a good mother.

My daughter started to tear at the paper on the examination table, pulling off a chunk and beaming, proud of herself, ready to thrust it into her mouth.

"Skulls are remarkably strong," the doctor continued. "I imagine she was more scared than hurt. No harm done."

But I didn't want her to be scared. It was my job to prevent fear, and I had failed miserably, all because I had selfishly craved both some time with other people and some time alone. All because I wanted that forty-five minutes of nap time when she didn't need me.

That evening I left my daughter and a bottle of pumped milk with my husband in the living room and retreated upstairs for a hot bath. I stripped off my sweaty clothes, stained with milk and baby food, smelling like my own neglect. And there, on my left hip, was a vibrant purple bruise where I had taken most of the impact of our fall, huge and throbbing with pain I had managed to suppress until I knew my daughter was okay.

"No harm done," I thought as I pressed into the bloom of it with my fingers.

Not too long ago a good friend of mine launched a new book at the same neighbourhood brewery where I had panicked years earlier over a red-hot wall-mounted heater. This beloved friend and neighbour had kept me company during those anxious and seemingly endless maternity leave days, had done laps with me and my baby around the park and listened to me unpack my postpartum neurosis. She showed up for me when my life shifted dramatically and didn't care that I was decidedly less exciting and infinitely more flustered.

I wanted to celebrate her, but the launch coincided with a day my husband was away on business, and we didn't have childcare on speed-dial. I can probably count on one hand how many dates I've been on with my husband in my daughter's lifetime, which is why when someone says "just get a babysitter" I feel the urge to burst into a fit of laughter.

After some scrambling, the mother of one of my daughter's classmates kindly offered to sit in my living room while I spent a couple of hours down the street raising a glass. There were some delays in putting my then six-year-old to bed, but I arrived at the launch thrilled that I'd managed to pull off this rare feat.

My friend was radiant that night, surrounded by the people who loved her and gracious when she gave a short speech about how the support of her community was the reason the book came together. I was so happy to be there but did eye the time, knowing the mother stationed in my living room watching reality television had her own family to get back to, her own demanding job to get up early for the next day.

As the evening started to wind down, I stood between two fathers, both writers themselves, one of very serious respected books and the other of very successful bestselling books. Each rhapsodized about how, despite their initial reluctance to have children, the love that came with having kids had definitely changed them for the better.

"You can't imagine your life without them," one opined, while the other nodded enthusiastically.

Inevitably the topic of children and work—specifically writing—reared its monstrous head, and the man to my right said something that nearly caused me to collapse onto the floor in the middle of the crowded bar.

"I don't know—I guess I didn't really find that my life changed all that much after having kids," he said.

These creative men whose "lives didn't change all that much" seemed to be everywhere after I became a mother. They published those books I couldn't finish writing, did radio spots I couldn't figure out how to make work, and wrote personal essays in (cough) women's magazines about the myriad rewards of fatherhood. They didn't seem to be derailed in the same way I was, and they shared that lack of derailment relentlessly on social media. They attended all the glamorous, high-profile literary parties and award ceremonies I was no longer invited to—notably without the mothers of their children by their side. Instead of chaos and terror, their personal identity shifts seemed only to bring them more respect, more accolades, and more work at a dollar-plus a word.

As I started to slowly claw myself out of the fog and back into a career, I noticed that the lives of so many of the men around me—my progressive husband included—were not nearly as disrupted by parenthood as mine was. Sure, many of them were tired, frustrated, and beleaguered, their freedom shaved off at the edges, but they largely came out of the chaos of those first few years unscathed in the long term. Not only that but the dads around me seemed to be thriving. Fatherhood provided them with a new kind of authority in the public sphere, a new appealing softness, an expanded perspective, one that was not offered to their mother counterparts.

Though my face was agreeable when the writer-father said "I didn't really find that my life changed all that much," the rest of my body reacted with a toxic, babysitter-less mix of resentment, jealousy, and rage.

Why was their experience so different? Had this culture that kept women fighting amongst each other distracted us from finding out?

In a rare moment during the first year of my daughter's life when I was not with her, I met a few old graduate school friends for drinks downtown. After diligently pumping and then kissing my daughter goodnight, I took the subway about a dozen stops, feeling like I had a severed limb, and settled in at the restaurant's bar almost an hour early, wanting to luxuriate in that rare solitude before dinner.

"It could have gone either way," one of them laughed when she arrived, finding me seated at the bar drinking a glass of Riesling alone. She leaned in to kiss my cheek. "Either you're always late because children have a way of doing that to you, or you're always early because you desperately need to get away from them."

This perfect little creature I had longed for who knew only need. I desperately had to both get away from and get back to her. I tried to reassure myself that this was all very normal, but it was hard not to feel like I was failing because, again, I wasn't like those mythical other mothers, the ones who loved being at home all day with their new babies. They cooed about the smell and the sweetness and the snuggles. They were glad to be away from their jobs, claimed that time was a thief, and only wanted to luxuriate in these early days forever.

Every direction I turned I felt like I could be doing better. That someone else was doing this better than me. That I was being looked at and judged the same way I had looked at and judged mothers before I became one.

But when that friend asked, I told her everything was going well. I remember she eyed me skeptically, with a small smile, but she didn't challenge my transparent assertion and I was nothing but grateful. I wanted to enjoy a meal out, to drink two glasses of wine without worrying obsessively about my breast milk, to walk down a street alone.

"No one really talks about how hard this time is," she finally said. She had three grown daughters and spoke from a place of genuine wisdom. "You can never say out loud you're struggling, because then you're seen as ungrateful."

I had wanted this for so long and certainly didn't want to be seen as ungrateful, but there was also a part of me that didn't complain, didn't reach out, because I had assumed the confounding loss of career and identity and sanity that came with motherhood only happened to other mothers. All those other mothers I had unfairly judged when I didn't know any better, other mothers who had been doing the best they could in a system that was never built for them in the first place.

Mostly I was embarrassed and ashamed about how wrong I had been.

It was always the small gestures of women, experienced mothers and the childfree alike, that buoyed me while I was drowning postpartum and beyond. In the early days, a Mason jar full of flowers, a care package of chocolate, a thoughtfully bagged collection of hand-me-downs. Later, a generous offer to just walk around the park or to sit in a song circle or to wait in my living room while I attended a book launch. Moments of tender reprieve, of thoughtful measured advice, and the simple permission to struggle and fail. Moments of recognition, moments of applause, moments of commiseration.

It took some time, but eventually I came to understand that those early whispered warnings from veteran mothers were not smug cautionary tales or opportunities for me to differentiate myself as "better." Instead, they represented generous permission to give myself grace. The women who candidly told me how hard it was to come back to the page, to come back to themselves, were—more often than not—really saying "it's okay to feel lost for a while, it's okay to simply loosen your grip and give it time, it's okay to not be doing great." They did so carefully but also with great kindness, acutely understanding how hard it was to find solid footing during that early physical, social, professional, and personal upheaval.

In those pre-birth stages of denial (and in those post-birth stages of self-flagellation), I failed to see the vulnerability and generosity of those other mothers. I didn't understand that they were carving out space for me to flounder and find myself in a way no one did for them, that they were being the voice of assurance they had desperately needed and never heard.

I didn't see it then but I see it now. I see so many things differently now.

When I am out in the world and see moms pushing strollers or with babies strapped to their bodies or seated on their beautiful handmade blankets in the park, some look so ethereal, so capable and perfect and together that it makes me want to scream "How?" over and over again into their meticulously made-up faces.

I wonder if any of them are as debilitatingly terrified as I was. I wonder if they feel like they're not doing a good job, are as broken and wounded and hapless as I was, yet are somehow hiding it. Do they miss who they were? Do they love who they've become? Do they long for the reprieve of nap time and wish life hadn't changed all that much?

I wonder how they do things so effortlessly, have enough confidence to accept that bad things will happen, that a mess will be left behind, that things will need to be sacrificed, but they will survive. I wonder how they don't all go mad with both the solitude and the lack of solitude, the all-consuming love that threatens to destroy them. How they don't refuse to accommodate, and why they don't take up even more space. How they offer no complaints despite the very real urge to scream. And scream. And scream.

I'm doing great, they all say. *I'm a good mom.*

And I wonder if they need someone to give them grace.

Little White Whale

hen I was younger, my ability to spontaneously and blissfully pass out anywhere and everywhere was legendary.

In my teens and into my early twenties, it became a joke among my friends that I could sleep through virtually anything—thunder storms, barking dogs, music cranked up to eleven, television blaring all night, conversations bubbling around me. During my first year of university, I famously fell asleep in the middle of a raucous three-floor dorm party, on a stained second-hand couch, nestled between scores of revellers and discarded beer bottles, the celebration of another Thursday night swelling around me.

No surface was too uncomfortable or unconventional. I could sleep in creaky living room chairs, on poorly blown-up air mattresses, and on generously provided floor spaces in strange apartments in faraway cities. I once, in true frat-boy fashion, fell asleep in a bathtub at a party. Sleep was my friend and I didn't need anything to consistently get it to come to me. Didn't need to coax it with chamomile, or ocean sounds, or blackout curtains. Didn't need an expensive prescription or witchy herbal supplement to turn off all the worry and dim the lights into a necessary oblivion.

Then, in my last year of university, I drank too many shots of tequila with a boy I had a deep, full-body crush on. After spending a fun-filled night at one of the city's seedier student bars, he invited me back to his apartment. We made ourselves something carb-heavy to eat and watched TV with his roommate.

Exhausted and ready to pass out, I asked him if I could borrow some pyjamas and stay the night, retreating to his bedroom alone while the two of them watched more television into the early post-bar hours.

I woke up later with him on top of me.

After that, sleep no longer felt safe and instead became elusive. After that, I was afraid to close my eyes. After that, I started sleeping with the light on.

It would be almost twenty years before I could comfortably fall asleep in the dark again.

Small children will make you sleep-obsessed in ways you never imagined possible. They will make you chase their naps like a gasping addict, walking or driving around town in aimless circles, playing tried-and-true narcotic music, or bobbing up and down and back and forth like a fool, both at home and in public. They will have you talking about sleep to any available stranger willing to listen, and calling ridiculously expensive sleep consultants, begging for help, crying into the phone.

(When my daughter was nine months old, I was so hysterical about sleep that my husband and I sat on a thirty-minute phone call with one professional who reacted to my desperation by telling me I should perhaps talk to my doctor about my own pressing mental health concerns.)

Small children will make you recite favourite sleepy-time storybooks from memory while pushing a stroller though a mall. They will have you standing, bleary-eyed, in a Toys R Us just before closing, spending money you don't actually have on swings and wraps and swaddles and some electronic thing called a Groclock that does little more than reveal an illuminated sun when wake-ups are "allowed." (My resourceful child eventually figured out how to turn on the sun by herself, regardless of what time it was.)

Small children will have you singing "Baby Beluga" over and over every night of the week until you want to claw your own eyes out.

Good night, little whale, good night.

My daughter had just turned two when the pandemic hit in 2020. Thanks to provincially adopted stay-at-home strategies, I had to say goodbye to the newly acquired autonomy childcare provided, the path from maternity leave back to working full time.

I was exhausted. Like many, my pandemic days were packed with a frantic, messy mix of parenting and paid work, and my pandemic nighttime rest was terrible. My inability to sleep was made worse by not moving all that much during the day, and the glass or two of harm-reduction wine before bed. As those arduous months wore on, I started to fall back on all those bad sleep-hygiene habits that had once made me feel safe: leaving the light, or the television, on throughout the night for company.

When that first COVID-19 summer turned to fall and the promise that things would get worse was fulfilled, I started having a recurring nightmare at least a few times a week. In the dream, I'm in my bedroom and the now-familiar sound of white noise from my daughter's sound machine drones away in the background while our old grey cat sleeps curled up at the end of the bed. The pale light from the bedroom window illuminates the doorway, creating ominous shadows that creep all the way down the hall.

And there was the man.

Dressed in an oversized army-green raincoat, he stands just outside my daughter's bedroom. His hood is pulled up over his head, partially covering his face. In his right hand, an indiscernible but obviously heavy object. He stands there motionless, rain shining from his slicker, dripping from his body, and pooling at his feet. He is an imposing statue threatening the unspeakable, an ominous stand-in for the anxiety I've felt most of my life.

But this time the threat wasn't to me. Every time, he would take a step toward my daughter's room. And then I would wake up.

Sometimes this dream would feel so real that I would actually get out of bed and check to make sure all the windows and doors were securely locked. (They always were, of course, but I had to check.) It would sometimes take me hours to get back to sleep—every errant sound from the floor below was, in my exhausted mind, that skulking stranger in the army-green raincoat. If I let my guard down even for a moment, that's when he would make his move.

I would pull the covers over my head. I would seek reassurance from my husband like a toddler terrified of whatever monster lurks in the darkness of her closet. Even though I know all of this is pretty absurd, the vision of him would persist whether I was sleeping or awake—a post-traumatic relic, soaking and still in the shadows, the weight of violence in his hand.

As much as I am a therapy evangelist, I don't think I need an hour-long session or two to decipher what this dream is really about. A mysterious threat lurking in the shadows, looking for a way into the safety of my home, ready to harm my family at any moment? That feels like a pretty on-the-nose pandemic metaphor. Surely my worried mind manufactured this faceless nighttime visitor in the army-green raincoat to stand in for my real-world worries—the kind I would need to suppress when I sent my daughter back to her newly opened daycare in the fall of that year with the pandemic still very much swirling around us.

It's as if my mind understands that my anxiety is now too much to carry during the day.

Here, it says. *Fear it all in the middle of the night instead.*

—

When I left the hospital after my daughter was born, I was instructed to have at least two Epsom salt baths a day to promote healing and soon became extremely grateful for the prescription. Once I grasped how elusive any kind of rest or solitude had become, it was a blessing to be given a genuine reason to retreat into the tub behind a locked door, to attempt to feel human again.

I would lie there in the warm water, my body ravaged by pregnancy and birth, all aching, loose and leaking, and while I was staring at all those new curves and folds, I would feel a reprieve from responsibility and actually *fall asleep for a brief moment or two*. With my daughter not directly in my care, tiny micro rests would overtake me like a crashing wave, my body deciding, without any input from me, that general weariness posed a greater risk than drowning. (I'm not entirely sure if this was more or less safe than falling asleep in an empty bathtub at a house party.)

The depths of that new exhaustion made my body ache in unfamiliar ways. There was a hollowness to me, deep behind my eyes, a pit I could never fill. Even when I was given an actual window to retreat ("sleep when the baby sleeps," they all said) I found that, despite how hard I tried and how tired I actually was, I simply couldn't find slumber. Instead I would just stare mesmerized at my baby's tiny fragile body, dimly lit in the bassinet next to my bed.

While I always seemed to be in a fog somewhere between sleeping and waking, my daughter slept in deep yet tiny demoralizing bursts. She was, in the language of sleep experts, a "catnapper." She had to be "trained."

And of course I had to do the training.

I want to preface everything I'm about to write with one fundamental, enduring truth: no one in the history of the world has been worse at sleeping than my child. I love her more than anything, and she's good at a great many things, but I can also confidently say she fucking sucks at sleeping.

Because of my daughter's early failures in the sleep department, I've read almost every available book on the subject and can tell you that there have been some ridiculous and even offensive opinions committed to paper. One expert opined that parents were simply "too obsessed with sleep," that they needed to learn to relax and "go with the flow." I assure you that the person who had this opinion did not have a baby who couldn't sleep more than forty minutes at a time, or who woke half a dozen to a dozen times throughout the night, or who eventually needed a multistep goodnight routine that resembled an elaborate musical theatre production. I can also assure you that this particular expert has never fallen asleep in a bathtub full of water, or underneath a play mat on their child's bedroom floor, or on a beloved stuffed turtle serving as a makeshift pillow.

When you're expecting a baby, friends, experts, and enemies alike will tell you—or rather, warn you—that sleep will be *an issue*. They will look at you with pity, as if you are about to be thrown to wolves that you believe to be puppies. You are going to endure the ultimate trial, and in your sweet naïveté, you still believe your life won't change all that much.

What these well-meaning but ultimately mocking experienced parents don't actually talk about is how the very concept of sleep will completely consume your life. You will become both an expert on it and a hapless idiot because of its lack, and you will lie in the hallway outside your child's room night after night making wishes and offering prayers for rest that will never be fulfilled.

My ability to properly rest left me in the final months of my pregnancy—during a time everyone told me to get as much as I could—and it didn't come back for years. While I wasn't sleeping,

I became completely consumed with the very idea of rest. The science of it. The impossibility of it. The necessity of it. The mocking unavailable flirtation of it. How much and how long I had taken it for granted.

I recently read that new parents won't actually pay off their accumulated sleep debt for up to six years, a horrifying claim that I entirely believe to be true. I still bear the scars and irrational behaviour of that early sleeplessness—still tiptoe around the house, avoid flushing the toilet after bedtime, and watch evening television on mute with subtitles. I am still never really able to achieve deep rest. Yet even as I write this, it feels futile to attempt to explain that level of sleep deprivation—and the desperation that erupts as a result—to anyone who has not experienced it. Now years out from those most extreme periods of sleeplessness, I'm not even sure I can entirely remember it properly myself.

What I do remember is people saying things like "you should really have a nap" and me wanting to punch them directly in the face.

During the first few years of my daughter's life, there were entire days when sleep (again, hers and mine) was the only thing I thought about, when all the things I previously cared about totally disappeared. Prior to her birth, I really had no idea that plans could be developed, or that complicated recordkeeping could be employed, to ensure my offspring not only went to sleep at preordained times but also stayed asleep for preordained lengths of time. I had no idea what "sleep pressure" was or what "wake windows" were, let alone that terms like these would make up my new doctrine. Nor did I understand that having my child stay awake for set periods of time would become just as important as getting her to drift off on her own in a dark room.

"Put the baby down *drowsy*, but not asleep" became very stressful law.

There were sophisticated schedules. There were four different white noise machines. The same story was read at the same time every day as a way of turning my child into a Pavlov dog salivating for sleep, a story that I can (still) recite entirely from memory.

And then there was *the song*—a sleep trigger that I still lean on today.

Good night, little whale, good night.

These complicated and exhausting tactics worked to varying degrees of success. But when one did and I was finally given a blessed window where I could tuck in, close my eyes, and drift off, I simply wouldn't be able to. A night feeding would predictably come at some ridiculous early-morning hour, and when it was over and she was finally sweetly asleep, I would return to bed and just stare at the ceiling. For hours. And hours. And hours. My whole body and mind were in a constant state of anticipation—probably an evolutionary benefit ensuring my baby's survival, but also something that had me teetering on the edge of madness.

All mothers are of course exhausted, but motherhood after forty brings its own unique brand of unjust fatigue. Your knees pop and creak, your back aches, you bend down and can barely get up, and you have a tiny sleepless person in your care all day long. I would wake up after only three or four hours of cumulative sleep and, despite how busy and exhausted I felt, have to fill oceans of time for my daughter's amusement or education or both. I would have to be inventive, and creative, and energetic, and patient. I would have to (always) be the best mom I could be, by whatever definition was currently prominent on the internet.

And while people talk a great deal about this concept of being "present in the moment," when it comes to finding the keys to mental health, happiness, and good parenting, no one really talks all that much about how exactly to achieve it. I mean, it seems simple enough—be in a particular moment and like it. But whenever I tried to totally focus on the thing at hand, a busy mess of thoughts came clamouring at the door like a herd of beasts. Those thoughts would thoroughly ruin the right now by promising something much needed in the future—sleep, an uninterrupted meal, some time to myself, new baby clothes in a size up—or they would unleash a flood of anxiety to ruin whatever pleasure could possibly be squeezed out.

Something more pressing or better or easier always seemed to be happening elsewhere, whether real or imagined, whether in time or place—regardless of how many people in grocery lines gave me unsolicited advice about how I should really treasure every moment, how I really should be grateful.

As if anyone could genuinely be this tired and grateful at the same time.

But there is a sick and twisted part of me that preferred that early sleep deprivation, spurred on by the pure adrenalin of being awake every hour, to the sleep deficit I'm now permanently running. That frantic dry-eyed desperate feeling of exhaustion actually kept me upright, the involuntary bathtub micronaps kept me going.

Now I am just really fucking tired all the time.

That boy I had a crush on in university apologized to me for what he had done.

The next morning the sun was coming in through the ratty curtains of his two-bedroom apartment, and we were sitting across from each other at his tiny dining room table, eating stale pastries and drinking black coffee. With a serious expression on his face, he told me he understood that what had happened the night before was wrong and that he would never do it again.

I wanted to go home. I forgave him. I have never really figured out if one thing was related to the other, but I knew, in the moment, it felt easier to say I forgave him.

"That's okay. I understand," I said, even though I probably didn't.

So many years later, I still think a lot about that boy. The one I had fallen so deeply in love with when I was barely an adult—with his beautiful angular face and awkward, hunched demeanour. The one whose bed I fell asleep in when I could still sleep.

Maybe I said I forgave him then when I really didn't, when all I really wanted to do was go home, when all I wanted to do was forget. But eventually that forgiveness would come to be true and I don't regret it now. I have learned that it is better to find peace with yourself than expect the just punishment of others.

So many years later, I think about that boy more than I should. I wonder what he's doing now, whether he has his own children, whether or not he sleeps at night. I think about how strange it is that we call them boys when, really, they are men. They are men enough to understand what they are doing, and that what they are doing is wrong. They are men enough to know they should apologize, even when they refuse to do so.

In my ever-light sleep, I have dreams about that boy, that *man*—not as ominous as my recurring pandemic dream with the man in the army-green coat, but in some ways just as haunting. They remind me how easy it is to love something that will harm you and how quickly, because it is easier, you will force yourself to forgive. How much you will try to forget.

But the dreams will always remind you.

I recently found a letter from that boy—that *man*—stored in a shoebox in the bottom of my closet, written more than twenty years ago and sent the summer after we finished university. Most relics of that time are gone now, but it's obvious why I decided to keep this particular letter. In it he apologizes for amorphous things—for not staying in touch, for not being "more," for not being there for me.

At the end he signs off, "I want you to know I think you're fabulous, but you already knew that."

I want him to know I never knew that.

During those sleepless nights, I memorized the contours of my ceiling. I became a student of methods to calm my own increasingly twitchy, terrified mind and stave off bad dreams. I did things that I never before imagined my cynical self doing. I meditated. I indulged in aromatherapy. I kept a vase of soothing lavender and a dish of blue, yellow, and purple crystals by my bed. I even downloaded an expensive sleep app and listened to Matthew McConaughey read me a bedtime story. (I'm not joking. It didn't work.)

The one thing that did finally work arrived entirely by accident: "Shipping Forecast," a utilitarian BBC Radio 4 broadcast of weather reports for the seas around the coasts of the British Isles. Issued by the Met Office, the United Kingdom's national meteorological service, and spoken in the wonderfully lulling accent of a British radio broadcaster, the weather and climate-related forecasts sound nonsensical to the untrained non-nautical ear, which is part of their sedative charm.

"Viking. Variable 4, becoming southerly 6 to gale 8," the near-monotone but very British voice in my headphones would recite in the middle of the night. "Moderate or rough, occasionally very rough later in north. Rain later. Good, occasionally poor. North Utsire. Variable 4, becoming southerly 6 to gale 8, perhaps severe gale 9 later. Moderate or rough, occasionally very rough later in north. Rain later. Good, occasionally poor."

The delightful evening narcotic that is the "Shipping Forecast" showed up one day when I most needed it, during a period of new motherhood when I was finding myself constantly awake between 1 a.m. and 4 a.m., likely doing nothing but scrolling through the 2016 pictures on a stranger's Instagram account. The broadcast wasn't sophisticated but rather the right blend of bland and beautiful, a sort of simple mundane poetry sending me right off to sleep within minutes, giving me a much-needed reprieve until the next nighttime crying jag wailed from the nursery and pulled me into its wreckage.

"South Utsire. Northerly 4 to 6, becoming variable 3, then southerly 5 to 7 later."

Terrible things do happen. There are unanticipated storms to fear in the night. Ominous horrors lurking in the shadows, soaking and still, the weight of violence in their hand.

"Moderate, occasionally rough. Rain later. Good, occasionally poor."

But for the most part, life is bland and beautiful.

Good night, little whale, good night.

It took me a few years and many phases of my daughter's sleepless life to finish this chapter, but the very week I started it, *she finally slept through the night for the very first time.*

In that airy quiet of morning, while the roar of ocean waves piped through the sound machine, I woke to find she hadn't yet stirred. My eyes opened in a rush of panic, my body rigid with anticipation, and then came the relief. Months of "training," of lying in hallways singing, of repeatedly reading sleepy-time storybooks, of walking the floor to operatic screaming, of breastfeeding and then breastfeeding and then breastfeeding again—it had all finally paid off.

She had actually managed to make it a full twelve hours without waking. She had done it. She could sleep.

Of course, even in victory, I knew that there would be so many more impossible moments in the future. Moments when I would feel afraid or hopeless or lost or hysterical. There will probably be ten of those today alone. It would seem that when it comes to children, every victory is followed by a thorough humbling, which keeps you small in the best ways.

I am still completely amazed that someone you love so completely can so consistently make you feel totally useless. And how that same person can so generously forgive you for your total uselessness. How after all the teary-faced dramatics of sleep training, she would blink her puffy eyes at me and smile, so happy to see the very person who had pleaded for a break and mercilessly shoehorned her into dreamland, and so thankful to be fighting all these ridiculous battles for sleep—and everything else—with me, together.

There is this thing that happens in the early mornings when my daughter wakes up from one of her restless nights. She will sigh and stir, looking for me to come and collect her. When she finally opens her eyes, she'll look around for a moment confused, scanning the space in front of her until she finally sees me. And as soon as she does, she will smile her big, adorable, goofy smile right at me.

And in that bland and beautiful morning moment, I am not afraid of anything.

The Python Pit

The horrors of the Inquisition are nothing compared to the fates your mind can imagine for your loved ones.

—Stephen King, *The Mist*

Early in my now twenty-year relationship with my husband, we adopted a dog from Toronto Animal Services. It was around the same time I was first diagnosed with anxiety disorder, a period of our lives when I was finding it difficult to leave the house, when I was groping for a solution to the beehive of worry in my broken brain. It was a nonsensical decision to add a damaged canine to the mix, but we did it anyway, completely taken by a badly behaved mutt we spotted on a walk through the shelter one weekend afternoon.

Shelby—the name she came with: a high-performance variant of the Ford Mustang, her namesake—was, initially, a total disaster of a dog. A stray for almost the entire first year of her life, reactive and destined for euthanasia, she somehow managed to convince shelter staff she was worthy of rehabilitation. She came into our home in a state of high-alert survival mode, living with what you might call a "scarcity mindset," believing every scrap of food, or safety, or freedom might be her last. She was protective and at times frankly terrifying—but right away I knew she was mine. I was immediately loyal to her without question, unwavering in my commitment to her recovery.

In our first year together, Shelby lunged at a maintenance man in the tight corridors of our apartment building when she assumed he was threatening me. (He wasn't.) She attacked another dog in a

Blockbuster Video when it surprised her coming around a rack of newly released *Da Vinci Code* DVDs. She was reported to building management for jumping up on someone in the elevator and got kicked out of two separate obedience schools—at one we were told that they were sorry but "there's nothing we can do to help her."

But when Shelby and I would walk together through our downtown neighbourhood and an interaction would inevitably trigger a disgusted passerby to shout "control your dog," I wouldn't feel embarrassed. Instead, I was proud she was getting better, if only in tiny increments. I was proud that we were working together toward something, even if we couldn't quite visualize yet what it would look like, even if it felt very far away.

For so long I had known shame, been fixated on the fact that people would see all the broken pieces of me just wandering around in the world, and tried desperately to hide them. And now here was this dog with all hers on full display, and I was the one who got to walk with her.

Four years after I first went into treatment for acute anxiety and panic disorder, four years after we adopted that anxious dog and attempted to rehabilitate her, my father had a pulmonary embolism.

An unanticipated complication after routine knee surgery, the blood clot that wandered into his lung sent him to the emergency room on a blazingly sunny day at the end of the summer I turned thirty-two. I didn't even know my father had been rushed to a hospital after complaining of massive chest pains until the day after it happened. My parents, very British and never very good at sharing a crisis—and knowing I was already an anxious type—didn't want me to be "worried."

At the time, I happened to be on the precipice of what I now know was the worst mental health crisis of my life, about to plunge into a deep depression that would push me back into the routine therapy I would continue for many years to come. I can't say if seeing my father on a gurney was the reason I fell off a cliff into a dark sea—that's an idea I didn't examine too deeply. It feels selfish to suggest his illness was my breaking-point, but it's certainly not unreasonable to assume that the idea of losing my dad was a catalyst, a knockout punch—I was already so vulnerable, struggling with anxiety and trauma and trying to keep it together day to day.

Whatever the reason, that summer a switch of sadness, already begging to be flipped, was flipped in me. While anxiety had long buzzed around me, depression was like an ominous scary movie monster that had been lumbering a few steps behind, waiting for me to stumble, for a circumstance to finally pounce and take me down.

The morning following my father's collapse, my husband drove me out to the suburban hospital. I remember throwing up in the parking lot before composing myself and going inside to see him. My robust, healthy father—a man who had needed the knee surgery because he had spent his younger days playing basketball and running marathons—lay small and vulnerable before me, dulled by drugs, pain, and embarrassment, shoved in a temporary bed in an ER horror show full of people in pain, a purgatory where he would remain for two more nights before a room of his own could be found.

I stood by his bedside with my mother and my husband in the busy chaos of the ward and watched as he groped for his words, listened carefully as he attempted to summon small requests through the thick fog of morphine. Could we speak to someone in hospital administration about finding him a room? Could we inquire about how long that might take? Could we get him a disposable bedpan? I could tell from the grey pallor of his face that the uncertainty of his situation was wearing on him, that he felt helpless in a way he never had before.

"This is very serious," an attending nurse told me in a private moment during that first miserable touch-and-go day. It seemed like a strange comment from a seasoned medical professional, a declaration that knocked me out of my own sense of sad resignation and spurred me into practical action.

One of the things that has long fascinated me about anxiety-prone people is how excellent we are in a genuine full-blown crisis. We may falter in the most innocuous situations, always obsessing about the arrival of the hypothetical worst-case scenario, but we thrive when that proverbial shoe drops—medical emergency, difficult birth, family tragedy, global pandemic. While I certainly find it hard to stomach any "anxiety is a gift" talk, I do admire myself for managing to be entirely capable when things go awry.

During those terrifying days my dad was in the hospital, I recall moving from detail to detail in a productive daze. Organizing insurance forms and drug prescriptions, future home visits and follow-up appointments. Finding the right people in the right offices and asking the right questions. Supporting my mother in the best way I could. And eventually the "very serious" worst-case scenario evolved into the best outcome.

My father was discharged and recovered completely. He became robust and active again, back to his daily three-mile walks and facing little more than the inconvenience of routine appointments. The blood clot turned out to be a random piece of bad luck and those scary summer days faded into a near miss we barely even talk about now—just the unanticipated static of life, an awful "remember when you almost died" moment that we somehow trudged through and cautiously but happily moved on from.

On the other hand, my fall into depression was not a random piece of bad luck or a near miss. The thick, sticky sadness that was ignited by that summer's very bad news followed me deep into the fall, suggesting that it had actually been coming for me for a long time. It had indeed been a beast lurking in the bush, watching and waiting for an opportune time to finally take me down. I'm not sure I fully understood the collapse until a concerned friend commented that I looked like I had lost a great deal of weight. I was capable of taking care of the finer details of my family's health crisis but incapable of taking care of myself.

Battling a monster of depression's ferocity meant the late-night interventions of close friends clutching takeout containers, a handful of tearful urgent-care appointments, and then a very lucky referral to an ongoing counselling program to address my history of sexual assault. I somehow managed to get onto a waiting list and then into a series of hour-long sessions in a windowless office with a very nice lady with a reassuringly kind face. I talked with her for hours in that lemon verbena–scented room lined with self-help books and inspirational posters. I unpacked the past for weeks and then months. We talked about the ways I had been harmed, the ways I had harmed myself, and the ways I had harmed others as a result.

Fall became winter and I began to miraculously clear away the shadows, learning how to cope not only with what had happened but also with whatever would come my way in the years ahead.

Via those sessions I was eventually referred to a specialist and assessed for and diagnosed with post-traumatic stress disorder. I'd of course already used the internet to catalogue my symptoms, with the growing fear that something was very wrong with me. I had weighed the stigma of being sick against the hope of finding relief. I'd gone back and forth again and again for years, and in that windowless hospital office, with its cheerful artwork and long, inviting pauses, I was finally given the room to say how I was feeling out loud—and the diagnosis gave me a place to start.

It turned out things were very serious, but it also turned out that I could—and would—get better.

For as long as I can remember—especially when I've faced particularly difficult bouts of anxiety—I've been drawn to being deliberately scared. I have, for example, always been the official roller-coaster rider in our family. My husband has long been firm on the fact that any ride that spins, lurches, or falls suddenly is off-limits for him, claiming a physical sensitivity that I find both incongruous to his entirely capable personality and totally adorable. Because of my love of a controlled scare, and because I am the only one with any interest in exhilaration, I'll usually sneak away alone during a day at the amusement park for a few turns on a thrill ride.

You would think that I would shy away from the scary. The whole point of flying around on barely safety-approved rails is to be temporarily terrified, and if you're prone to exploring worst-case scenarios, the news is never in short supply of coaster-related disaster stories. But I like my entertainment to excite, horrify, and even disturb, something that may seem illogical given my history of being full-body horror-stricken for no good reason—or maybe something that is entirely reasonable.

I track my obsession with a good scare back to an early-teens basement sleepover screening of *Night of the Living Dead*. I was immediately enthralled as Romero's black-and-white zombies ambled toward the camera while their human foils recoiled in terror. Eventually Michael Myers lingered in suburban shadows and Freddy Krueger popped up in dreams, while Jason (and his overbearing mom) terrorized hordes of horny would-be camp counsellors. As a nineties teen, I benefited from the glossy slasher boom that followed Wes Craven's *Scream*, feasting on final destinations, and urban legends, and whatever it was they did last summer.

In his 2024 collection of horror film criticism *Glowing in the Dark*, Orrin Grey writes, "The things that really scare me aren't that interesting. They're banal, boring, and quotidian. Like most people, I'm afraid of failure, of financial hardship, of getting sick, or letting my loved ones down. The really scary things in life don't put your heart in your throat and get your blood pumping; they just weigh you down, day after day, like being pressed under stones, one stone at a time, any one of which would be nothing at all, all of which added together crushes the air from your lungs and makes every breath agony. Those are the things that scare me, but I sure as hell don't want to write about them. I'd rather write about monsters."

As I got older, I continued to luxuriate in the therapeutic exercise of controlled terror via the big and small screen, shielded my eyes and plugged my ears when I had to, and temporarily numbed myself to the real-life horror Grey describes. I was comforted as fictional detectives uncovered the motives of brutal serial killers; I delighted in watching Jack Nicholson's axe come through the bathroom door or Johnny Depp getting gobbled up by his own bed. Horror allowed me an escape from having to think about being pressed under all those stones. It also had a way of freeing me from the fear of them.

Terror, no matter how it is consumed, is all about working through things. My personal obsession with being deliberately scared is more about what I need to process than what is actually happening in the plot du jour. When I see Laurie Strode attempt to defeat a knife-wielding maniac with a knitting needle and a wire coat hanger, I have renewed faith that I can actually be the final girl in my own personal horror show. I can temporarily suspend my pervasive disbelief in myself. And that's the point.

Despite the keep-you-up-at-night scares, the fiction of horror actually makes us feel safer. It buoys and inspires to see others strive for survival in the worst of circumstances. There is something very human about wanting to see people hang on so desperately to life and fight their way into the light as the darkness seeps in.

For the longest time, I believed myself to be afraid of everything. That I was incapable and needed to be coddled, needed to be catered to, couldn't withstand life's changes or challenges. Watching horror in its many incarnations became a way to prove that enduring narrative dead wrong. The assumptions I made about myself, about what I could handle, could be obliterated when I voluntarily sat through—and enjoyed—a campy seventies slasher, a perfectly timed James Wan jump scare, or Buffalo Bill taunting Catherine Martin from the top of the pit he's imprisoned her in. Horror was an arena for me to prove that, regardless of what other people thought of me and what I thought of myself, I was not, in fact, afraid of everything.

If a teenage babysitter could successfully subdue her own relentless boogeyman then, surely, I could quell those anxieties that had been stalking me. Surely, I could face the worst.

The year my daughter turned four, we took her to a small amusement park in Owen Sound, Ontario. Thanks to two preceding pandemic years, it was her first summer ever that included an amusement park, so in the week beforehand I diligently researched all the rides on-site, making sure there were enough appropriate for her size. The website promised a slow-moving train, a tractor ride that explored a "farm" (complete with live chickens and goats), and kid-sized blue and yellow boats with clanging bells on their bows. Perhaps most exciting was a tiny "rocket ride" that swung in graceful circles as it lifted children off the ground.

My daughter was enthusiastic, but a little nervous. Back when she was a baby, a wise friend of mine had told me that "as they grow older, children reveal to you who they always were." It remains probably the most accurate piece of information anyone gave me during that challenging early time. My daughter revealed herself to be thoughtful and, well, a little apprehensive about everything from playground slides to cheese quesadillas.

While other children threw themselves headlong into action, my daughter would often wait cautiously on the sidelines, sussing things out, gathering information, considering the scene. She would linger on the edge of a playground or wading pool, pause before crawling into the playgroup fray. She wasn't shy exactly, but reserved—maybe even a tiny bit suspicious—assessing thoroughly and figuring out just the right moment, *her* moment.

That ability to stay put and observe until the right time translated into being a late walker. Though I fretted that there might be something wrong developmentally, in reality she just couldn't see the point in getting on her feet and wandering somewhere else. My own physiotherapist told me that it was nothing to worry about, that if we got to eighteen months and she hadn't taken a few steps to bring her in then for an exam. (My daughter was reluctant right up until that deadline, eventually walking at seventeen months and twenty days.)

I admired my daughter for being discerning—a trait I didn't have myself—but for obvious motherly reasons I also worried about her being too cautious. I worried that my near-lifelong ability to fret about things, to hold myself back, had indeed rubbed off on her and flourished into an apprehension that meant she was missing out.

I worried that she had inherited my worry.

When we went to that amusement park on a sunny day in August, the air was cool and the park not too busy. We fed eager deer from our palms, ate salty French fries from cardboard boxes, and played a round of minigolf. The lines were sparse for the train and the tractor, and my daughter happily floated around in her tiny kid-sized boat, clanging its big metal bell while I took a thousand photographs.

But when it came time for the rocket ride, there was that characteristic trepidation. As we approached, I watched the other children spin in circles, squealing with delight, and remembered what all the parenting books had advised.

Encourage your children to try new things, even if they are afraid. Mould them into brave and adventurous beings. Raise them to be resilient, intrepid adults.

"It'll be fine, honey. We'll be right here."

The sullen teenage attendant, barely over sixteen and wanting to be elsewhere, buckled my daughter into her swinging red-and-blue rocket and sauntered casually back to the big red start button. The other children shrieked and waved at their moms and dads, shaking their own rockets back and forth as they impatiently waited for things to get started.

With an abrupt jerk my daughter's rocket crept forward, moving slowly at first but then picking up speed into a hypnotic, whirring spin. Her face crumpled. She began to panic. She called out for me and I helplessly told her it would be okay. She began to cry quietly. I began to panic.

"I can stop it," the teenage attendant said in emotionless monotone.

"Yes. Please," I begged.

Mould them into brave and adventurous beings. Raise them to be resilient, intrepid adults.

Surely I had hovered too much when she was a baby; checked the car seat straps too many times; been too worried that she would choke on grapes or fall in her new shoes, that the room was too hot or too cold, that she would somehow be snatched from me when I wasn't diligently building a fortress of concern around her.

I collected her up in my arms and held her close. I told her it was okay. I told her I was sorry. I told her we could go home.

My mother once said that when she found out she was pregnant with me she got down on her knees and prayed I wouldn't turn out like her. She has never elaborated on what she meant by that, what specific character traits she hoped I would dodge in the great linked chain of inevitable heredity, but once I was pregnant with my own child I understood her sentiment completely.

Every flaw and foible, every hateful, painful thought, every bad habit and behaviour, every moment of self-imposed suffering embedded in the genetic code, and then potentially burned beneath the skin via hovering nurture.

Of course I didn't want my daughter to turn out like me. I didn't want her to grow up terrified of unknown incoming calls or routine blood tests, of dinner party invitations or public speaking or social media follow requests, of crowded rooms or other people's potentially nefarious (but probably just fine) intentions. I didn't want her to hate her body and starve it accordingly; or have a panic attack in the office bathroom at work; or spend a not insignificant chunk of her late twenties secluded inside her apartment, afraid to get on the elevator, see a concert, or go to a bar with friends. I didn't want her to keep the vibrancy of life at a safe distance, thinking that by doing so she was keeping sadness, hurt, and mayhem at bay. (I have learned that sadness, hurt, and mayhem will always find you no matter how hard you try to keep them at bay.)

I wanted my daughter to climb trees and jump off tire swings and dive headfirst into life. I wanted her to gleefully get on the rocket ride and scream and scream and scream with absolute delight. I wanted her to ask to go again.

The following summer, at that same Owen Sound amusement park, my daughter insisted on upgrading her personal ride resumé to include something called the Python Pit, the park's only roller coaster.

Having just finished junior kindergarten, her social circle and subsequent sphere of knowledge (and influence) had expanded outside the warm fuzzy primary-colour confines of preschool. She had friends who bragged about their amusement park prowess, one adventurous girl in particular claiming to have ridden a roller coaster multiple times. (Which roller coaster and how many times exactly was unclear.) I couldn't be certain, but it seemed my daughter wanted to go back to senior kindergarten that fall with the same claim and related bravado.

She too wanted to brag about being unafraid.

My daughter's previous rocket ride experience meant I was surprised by her insistence to ride the Python. I even tried to gently caution that maybe it wasn't for her. But after some discussion, the two of us squeezed in at the back of the train, her tiny body snuggled close to mine as yet another sullen teen with a boring summer job strapped us safely in.

A single train with five cars that arranged riders two across in a single row, the steel coaster was painted a garish neon green with a cartoonish snake head protruding from the front. Categorized as a "family coaster," it had a relatively minor eleven-and-a-half-foot drop and even permitted children shorter than thirty-six inches to ride with an adult. My husband waved from the ground, successfully hiding his own trepidation, his face only conveying how proud he was of her for trying. He was smiling. She was smiling. I'm sure I was too.

But as we climbed to the first escalation, I could feel that familiar fear rise in her body—the anticipation, the creeping terror, the regret over the decision to be wilfully scared. Predictably, after one rotation in the Python Pit my daughter had absolutely had enough. She decided that she was ready to go back to the comfort of tractors and trains and boats with bells on the bow.

The teenage attendant made eye contact with me, offered an expression of knowledgeable sympathy as we whizzed by him, his friendly, helpless shrug indicating this time there was no stopping the ride to get off. This time we just had to muddle our way through it.

"But I want to get off," she said to me, her eyes ablaze.

I would see that fear on her face again the following winter when the two of us went to a sold-out afternoon screening of *The Wizard of Oz* at our local rep cinema. When the tornado lifted Dorothy's house into the sky, she declared—*loudly*—that she needed to leave. *Now.* When I resisted, tried to haplessly "build her resilience" by telling her that everything would be fine soon, she quite rightly pushed back.

"You promised we could leave if I got scared," she said.

From our vantage point in the lobby, peering through a tiny window in the cinema door, we watched Dorothy's house land with a thud and the movie shift dramatically into technicolour—the very moment she felt safe enough to go back in.

Unlike a movie theatre, you can't leave a roller coaster. You have to simply let it run its course. And as our neon-green car slowed and dipped into the brief calm before the next ascent, I knew there were a whole two more laps left for her to endure.

Her panic became my panic. I had failed at my job. I hadn't warned her enough. I hadn't protected her from being afraid.

Sometimes I am anxious about how much of my life I have lost to dealing with anxiety. The things I didn't try, the places I didn't go, the people I didn't meet. Anxiety cruelly cuts off various avenues of your existence, traps you in what you wrongly believe is a tiny sphere of safety, makes you mistrust yourself and your reality. I often wonder what opportunities didn't come my way because I was too afraid to come out of that hole I had dug for myself.

There was no magical solution to my anxiety. Wellness was, of course, a lot of fucking work. It was a slow-moving and arduous process that involved a lot of daily diligence. Enough sleep. Enough to eat. Enough exercise. Enough social contact. The thoughtful consideration of why I thought the way I did, and the arduous endeavour to retrain. Talking and workbooks and analysis and insufferable self-reflection.

But being upright after experiencing many years of debilitating worry—and then months of severe depression—was entirely exhilarating. *Wellness was exhilarating.* In contrast to the dark days that had come before, those terrifying moments where death felt like a viable option, life felt like a pop song on the radio. Like Dorothy in Oz, I peered through the open door and the world was suddenly in full colour, the mix of terror and apathy that had long consumed me moving out like a dissipating fog. I had been the walking dead and now I was so very alive.

In the year that preceded my decision to become a mother, mental health itself seemed to arrive all at once—like a light coming on in a long dark room, or a new pair of glasses that suddenly helped you see. What had been stolen from me—those various avenues of existence I had been too sick and scared to pursue—had suddenly been returned.

In the wake of that change, I took on work that brought me joy and felt like the words I was writing were making an impact, that they meant something to someone. I fell deeply in love with all sorts of new things, and back in love with all sorts of old things, including baseball and, as a consequence, writing about it.

I had ambition. I decided to do a master's degree. My husband and I decided to renew our vows in Las Vegas. We decided we would try to have a baby.

There was something better in the future—even if we couldn't quite visualize it yet, even if it felt far away—and we were moving toward it.

The roller coaster ascended for the second time, its anticipatory "click click click" likely only heightening the very real horror my daughter was experiencing, trapped in the inevitably that we would fall again, that the car would clip around its rickety track another time, and then another time.

While the people around us shrieked and laughed, my helplessness mirrored my daughter's—there was no way I could change her current circumstance. I wrapped my arm around her and leaned in close to her ear.

"Do you know what always helps me when I'm really scared?" I asked over the roar of the rails. My face was as calm, reassuring, and placid as I could manage. (The thing I've learned about children is that they can always sense your uncertainty.)

She looked up at me, not speaking. She was waiting for the answer from the person who was supposed to give her all the answers.

"I scream real loud," I quickly told her. "As loud as I possibly can. It helps. Can you do that for me?"

She nodded cautiously. The roller coaster had nearly reached the top and she gripped my hand tightly. As it spilled over the edge, she opened her mouth and let go.

That reactive, anxious disaster of a dog passed away not too long ago. She was what many would refer to as my "heart dog," with me through all those aforementioned good and bad days, through my dad's trip to emergency, my deep depression, through infertility, through the birth of my daughter and her early years, through the loss of and then reformation of my identity.

If I'm honest, Shelby never *entirely* recovered from her scarcity mindset. In fact, she is now infamous for stealing and eating a bizarre list of things: a pound of butter, six corncobs, a jack-o'-lantern, an eighteen-dollar brick of Parmesan, an entire take out container of chana masala, and another dog's tennis ball (that one had to be surgically removed). She also never fully recovered from her aggressive distrust of other dogs, or the mail carrier, or tractor trailer trucks.

My daughter was four years old when kidney disease took Shelby from us, but I'm grateful they got to spend the final years of that canine life together. Watching them side by side reminded me that Shelby's beautiful, long life wouldn't have happened if we hadn't put in the work, if I hadn't always been proud to walk with her, if I hadn't shelved the shame and believed healing was possible. While I endeavoured to make Shelby's snarling anxiety manageable over time, I also managed my own and—despite my worst fears—discovered that maybe I wasn't just the story of my anxiety. Maybe I wasn't destined to pass that anxiety down to the child who enthusiastically loved her very good dog without judgment.

Trying to keep a child safe while also giving them the freedom and confidence to adventure and explore is an impossible calculus. As my daughter grew out of baby clothes into toddler sizes, zoomed on shaky legs around coffee tables and kitchen chairs, my greatest personal challenge was trying to figure out exactly how much hovering was too much hovering, and which of the thousand things I was near-constantly told to worry about warranted my actual attention.

In my time as a parent, I have been told to be terrified of trampolines, sleepovers, scented candles, Crocs on escalators, forgoing family dinner, screen time, Minecraft, microplastics, and red dye No. 3, but most often I have been warned to "just relax." The line between appropriately concerned (a "good mother") and crazy (a "very bad mother") always seemed so imperceptibly fine, and I gritted my teeth through countless playground and playdate scenarios that set my over active worry meter ablaze.

After all, one of the things a mother needs to worry about most is making her child a lifelong worrier.

While the standard paranoia that a child can be "ruined" by concern runs amok, the truth is: worry is normal, and common, and can even be helpful. A fear of peril can and often does keep us and others safe, sometimes without us even realizing it. What is damaging is when it goes unquestioned and unchecked, when it turns to catastrophic thinking, when your worry bosses you around to the point that you cannot enjoy life. In some ways, excessive worry is less a flaw and more an entirely necessary tool wielded incorrectly—a product of what you have experienced.

Anyone who has successfully subdued the monster that is anxiety will tell you that overcoming it is not actually about *not* being afraid. For the longest time I assumed that to be well I needed to be entirely fearless—even reckless. Instead, recovery is about understanding that yes, there is a universe of terrible things that *could* be coming—cancers and car crashes, break-ins and boogeymen—but they're not necessarily coming *right now*. Loss is inevitable, and the potential for loss grows beyond your wildest imaginings when you become a parent. Somehow you must teach yourself to not let the "what if" taint the right now. You learn to take a deep breath and somehow enjoy the moment.

And because there is no real escape from suffering, no way to know if or how it is coming for us, when exactly it will step out from the shadows, we must find a way to cope. We must find safe ways of looking directly at the things we fear the most, if only so they won't destroy us. The way to deal with fear, with suffering, with pain is not to keep it in, stuff it down, suffocate it with a thousand repetitions of "no really, it's okay, I promise."

The way to deal with it is to start screaming.

Trauma taught me that. Infertility taught me that. Motherhood taught me that.

When I think about what it means to parent with anxiety, I try not to be afraid that this stain I've tended to for so long will rub off on the one person I want so much to keep safe and well. Though I can work hard at it, do my best, anxiety is yet another thing I simply cannot shield her from if it's destined to come. Fear, in its various degrees and incarnations, comes for all of us eventually.

Yet perhaps instead of passing down to my daughter my own penchant for worry, I am giving her everything I have learned to cope with it. I am giving her the voice to challenge it, the tools to dismantle it, the lack of shame I didn't have.

Perhaps I am teaching her to scream.

My daughter gripped my hand and screamed as hard as she could that day on the Python Pit. She screamed until her screams became laughter and the ride finally ended. (She did not want to go again.) She still talks about how she rode that roller coaster—how she hated every moment of it, yes, but she rode it. Her complete dislike transformed into the kindergarten brag she wanted, a badge of bravery that still assures her she can do hard things.

Before we left the amusement park, my daughter insisted on one final ride. She wanted to get back on the rocket.

"Are you sure, honey?" I asked, playing supportive but feeling reluctant, remembering her fear on the roller coaster only moments before, her fear on the rocket the year before.

She nodded staidly and joined the short line, soon ushered onto her very own red-and-blue rocket ship by a teen as sullen and checked out as the one who had pushed the big start button the summer before.

"Are you sure?"

Another nod.

As the ride began to jerk awake, I saw that familiar look—familiar to her but also familiar to me. It was a look that has found its way onto my face countless times in countless situations over so many years since that first panic attack. I saw my face in hers, anxiety as hereditary, the knowledge that there is no escape. That place where panic begins, the root of it, where it swings up to eventually swirl into a tornado. I resisted the very real urge to ask the attendant to simply stop things, just as her predecessor had volunteered to do a year earlier.

But after one rotation I realized my daughter was repeating something to herself over and over again. Her worry seemed to abate. There was no crying this time around. She was in a place all her own as the ride spun in circles, the other children laughing and screaming.

After a dozen spins on the rocket ride the machinations slowed and the sullen teen made the rounds unclipping safety harnesses. She opened the gate and I ran in to pull my daughter from her seat, trying hard not to hold her too close before I placed her feet back on the ground.

She smiled up at me.

"What were you saying to yourself out there?" I asked.

"I'm going to be okay," she said.

Forgetting and Being Forgotten

Towards the end of the first year of my daughter's life, my husband and I were able to figure out a pocket of time so I could have one luxurious day a week to myself. I hadn't written anything substantial since the second-last month of my pregnancy and was increasingly worried that if I didn't at least get something done I would not only lose work momentum but also go slightly mad. So, in the interest of creating space for me to dip back in, my husband would stay home from the office on Thursdays, dealing with any of his own work fires during my daughter's naps, and I would kiss the two of them goodbye and go out into the world alone.

We called it "daddy-daughter day." (Not that we called every other weekday "mommy-daughter day." Those were just "days.")

I would leave the house on Thursday morning and walk to a busy nearby coffee shop, the library, or one of my postpartum appointments. I missed having my own office (the cat was certainly enjoying it), but I liked navigating the outside world after spending my daughter's early days in bedridden recovery. I would run errands or do any small pieces of work I had managed to scrounge up from my now eerily quiet email account. As I did so, I would always be struck by the immense feeling of freedom, the idea that my body was suddenly my own. Each foot hit the pavement without the worry that came from having a person attached to me, each decision with the focus of being responsible only for myself in the moment.

No one knew I was a mother. I was a mystery again.

Early on in my writing career, I was accepted into a literary non-fiction writing program. It offered a paid opportunity for a month away from my nine-to-five "real" life to focus on a single long-form essay and "learn about the craft" in a beautiful locale with brilliant mentors and the camaraderie of classmates.

I felt deeply out of place in the program. While I was an experienced writer with a few published novels and an agent who had agreed to represent me, back home I had a full-time magazine desk job—one that did not involve writing for a living—and I was trying desperately to create a literary career in the few off-hours away from a demanding employer. I was a non-fiction novice, leaning on my newspaper book reviews and a handful of magazine bylines to get in. My lack of formal journalistic training meant the feeling of being an imposter followed me into those writing rooms: I was terrified that the largest writing project I'd ever embarked upon in this genre would simply be too much for me to handle.

The piece in question was a memoir about what it was like to grow up in the Toronto suburb where the notorious Paul Bernardo lived, back when he was known only as the "Scarborough Rapist." It required countless hours of disturbing research, emotional interviews with residents, and a deep dive into the fear a community tried to forget. Every day I would go to my tiny cabin in the Alberta woods—a beautiful, rugged writing studio with floor-to-ceiling glass windows that allowed for the occasional deer sighting—and sit in a stew of trauma, trying and failing to achieve any emotional distance.

In my first draft, the one that would be workshopped by peers and pored over by mentors, I mentioned that I myself had been assaulted as a young teen—a dark night on a date so many years ago that I had largely tried to forget. I'd mostly succeeded, though it was a night that had nonetheless shaped me, my worldview, and my mental health.

"What happened?" one mentor—a highly respected and decorated male journalist—wrote in the margins. "Expand." "Needs more."

We need more information here.

I read through all the editor's notes on that early draft, and then I lay on my back on the floor of my cabin in the woods and cried. I decided I couldn't do what was required of me to be a successful non-fiction writer, couldn't unearth what was necessary to make a story compelling, couldn't poke at wounds, whether mine or anyone else's. I remember calling my agent, telling her all these things I couldn't do, and I remember her kindly telling me *I didn't have to*, that she would support me regardless.

Now, with many more years of experience writing and editing non-fiction, I can see the necessity to keep things private between one line and the next, can see that the paragraphs not written belong solely to the writer. I can see all the things readers—and therefore editors and publishers—demand we expose for the sake of narrative, the revelations that translate into clicks and therefore profit, the things we desperately need to blot out for the sake of our own precious sanity. The things that we have a right to say no to, the things deliberately forgotten so we can survive.

There are definitely good reasons to write about trauma—in its purest form, self-expression is indisputably healing, and when shared, that expression can create community, provide solace, and shine a much-needed light on oft-misunderstood experiences and oft-ignored issues. The impulse to write about the most painful corners of our personal and social histories is a perfectly natural one, but in the modern world, that process inevitably bumps up against a fear of feeling exposed, or shamed, or a stranger simply knowing more about you than you would really like and the subsequent judgment that may invite. The act of writing about your own violation always sets those two opposite forces in conflict—the need to let it all out, let it go, and make something good from it versus the very human need to keep yourself safe, to live vibrantly beyond how you have been harmed, to define yourself on your own terms.

In my cabin in the woods, I eventually acquiesced to that desperate need to express, gave the reader—and therefore the editor—what they wanted. I went to dark places, mined the details, and unearthed what was necessary to tell a compelling story. By the end of those thirty days I had written ten thousand words, the editor in question signing off on successful completion. Eventually published in a shorter form, the piece was one I was proud of. But, as my initial inner conflict suggested, I was not wholly ready for the attention it garnered, a part of the writing process I still struggle with today.

Though it was written over ten years ago, that piece still comes up from time to time. There will be a news item that triggers a share on social media, or someone will dig it up and email me about it. People will bring it up at bars or parties, in casual conversation.

I have to wonder: Why would they think I would want to discuss my deepest trauma, my earliest wound, with them, a stranger? Why would I want to go back?

After my daughter was born, after I had finally accepted that airline travel and eight-hour-plus workdays were no longer a viable option, I experimented with the opposite of that in-depth disclosure and subsequent hypervisibility: forgetting and being forgotten. The timing was perfect, because disappearing is exactly what the world asks of you when you become a mother.

In its current under-resourced incarnation, motherhood dictates that you step away socially, culturally, sexually, professionally. (It also requires you to bounce back like said retreat never happened.) For me, the requirement of stepping away was jarring but not altogether unwelcome. Though the sexlessness, the invisibility, the exclusion, the derision was certainly distasteful, I was not entirely opposed to the end product: a quieter life.

In fact, I was determined to breathe a sigh of overdue relief and readily embrace it.

Making noise in this particular era requires a certain stamina for abuse, whether you write about sports or social issues or tuna noodle casserole. At the time of my daughter's birth, I had none left. I was tired of dodging sexist vitriol from strangers online because of even the most innocuous things (a defence of baseball's intentional walk in our national newspaper once garnered me an excessively long email from a reader about just how *fucking stupid* I am). When I was finally able to leave my office job and become a full-time writer, I was basically standing in an open field, unprotected by editors or publishers, while strangers threw insults at me.

I didn't want to be so public anymore. In short, I was over it.

I also thought that disappearing would keep my daughter safe, that if I attracted no attention, she would be protected from harm during our most vulnerable time. It was fine to endure the trolling and threats when it was only me (actually, it was never fine), but now it made more sense to disappear in aid of security.

(Are we even able to really disappear in this world that we have created? Have we ensured that we will always be found by all that *more information* we have left behind, by what we have excised and left out in order to heal?)

Despite how much I missed aspects of my old life, I felt the pull to be with my daughter entirely, to put my notebook and my dreams away in a desk drawer and temporarily forget all about the busy world that used to totally control and consume me. While the desire to put words on the page never left me, I wanted to be present and felt increasingly compelled to disappear and retreat and enjoy our sacred covenant of two. I temporarily pushed my old life from view and instead fixed my gaze on her while she slept in my arms.

But there is a problem with disappearing, willing yourself to be forgotten, even for a short period of time: it becomes very hard to come back.

Reflecting on the early days of her career as a film critic, Claire Dederer writes, "I somehow was never able to transcend the sense that I was an audience member, rather than a professional." In many ways that's how I felt about my seven-year pre-baby foray into baseball writing—and apparently how others felt about it too. When I promoted my book on the game, the media repeatedly called me a "superfan," especially when I was slotted on a live panel or sharing a radio spot with a "real" (often white male) baseball expert. I came to learn it was all the *feelings* that made me a fan—loving something could never be professional. (Though interestingly enough, hating something could be.)

And yet even with this insecurity, while still on unofficial maternity leave, I interviewed for a full-time sports writing job. I think in my heart I knew it was an ill-advised plan, but I still felt this longing to participate and be seen again. In many ways this was my dream job—at least the type of dream that I'd had before I became a mother.

Almost immediately the process of even applying felt impossible with an infant in my full-time care, but buoyed by a few kind friends in journalism who said they thought I'd be perfect for the role, I pushed on. I was elated to be shortlisted for an interview, but when the human resources rep told me the process involved receiving a "surprise" assignment via email that I'd be asked to return within twenty-four hours, I was levelled by my own reality.

Writing an insightful column within a twenty-four-hour period necessitated childcare I didn't have. I was honest with the rep, asking if he could please let me know an exact timeframe so I could get my husband to take the day off work, giving me a block of time to complete the assignment. That very kind man did me a (perhaps unsanctioned) favour simply by letting me know when the email would arrive.

The surprise assignment should have been my first clue. The writing world, and pretty much the entirety of the working world in general, is not designed for parents of small children (or caregivers of any kind) under the best of circumstances. It's not designed for daycare drop-offs and pickups, for school drop-offs and pickups, or for the countless sick days necessitated by the myriad diseases a child seems to get in the first years of their life. (Hand, Foot, and Mouth Disease! Fifth Disease! Ear Infections! Ear Infection Antibiotic Reactions!) It's certainly not designed for people who are recovering from any seismic mental or physical shifts, who experience any subsequent mental health issues, who have to attend to a 5 p.m. dinner hour and a 6:30 p.m. bedtime, or who sleep in dismal three-hour chunks.

And yet I pushed against this ugly reality long enough to write the "pretend" column as requested. I then went to the scheduled interview in the highly corporate building, nervously sitting in the editor's tiny office in front of three fantastically well put together working people who did not seem to be worrying about dinner or bedtime or daycare pickup or fifth disease.

Though I'm sure that in reality the meeting was just fine, in my mind it was a disaster.

The entire experience of that interview was a particular harsh-reality low point of early parenthood for me. It solidified the creeping realization that all those pre-baby promises of "we can make it work" were actually hollow, that if I somehow managed to continue the work I loved I would rarely see my daughter and live in a perpetual state of high stress and little to no sleep. Even if the world made good on its promise that I could go back to the way things were, milestones would be missed and sacrifices would have to be made.

If I had wanted to "make it work" at that job, I wouldn't get the chance—the hiring committee didn't even call to let me know I'd been passed over. (I found that out by seeing the successful candidate's headshot in the publication about three months later.)

One of those kind friends who had encouraged me offered a conciliatory "well, it was really good that you applied."

Was it good that I felt foolish for even attempting to hold on to my old life? Was it good that I felt like the interviewers were looking at me like I was an adorable dog who was trying, unsuccessfully, to walk and talk? Was it good that on my way home I sat down in the city's central train station and cried, perhaps out of humiliation, perhaps out of grief over the death of my old life, perhaps because new motherhood had been so hard and I had felt so helpless?

The interview and the very public cry that followed set the tone for subsequent attempts to return to a world I felt had left me behind. At the end of my daughter's first year, I realized that by becoming a mother I had fallen out of my old reality, and there was no obvious way back in.

In her memoir *Ambition Monster*, recently reformed workaholic Jennifer Romolini reflects on that inexplicable longing to participate and be seen. "Even more than becoming a writer, I dream of becoming a somebody," she writes. "Of achieving success that is unambiguous, the kind that lets the world know you're okay, that you made it, that you're better than they all thought you were. The kind that might make you feel that way about yourself, too."

During those daddy-daughter days when I found a bit of freedom, I would always prioritize a meal in a restaurant alone. Even though caregiving meant I spent significantly less time socializing, I always felt like it was more important to spend a lunch hour with myself than with anyone else. I would often pick the day's restaurant based on the ability to order something that would be hard to eat with a baby in your care. Piping hot ramen. A sloppy pasta dish. Messy overfilled tacos. Sometimes I would order an extravagant cocktail, but often just a glass of wine. Lush, juicy, bold French reds. Five ounces, sometimes nine. One glass, sometimes two. More expensive than I would normally allow myself.

Those lunches felt a great deal like I was having an affair with my former self. An amorous union with the person who occasionally stayed out too late and enjoyed a good egg white cocktail. The person who always knew where the good restaurants were and had the income to eat at them. The person who carried a purse not a backpack; who left the house without diapers, and wipes, and emergency snacks; who didn't worry about when the last feeding or where the nearest change table was.

A person with a certain kind of freedom that she had taken for granted.

Interestingly, when I told other mothers about this weekly ritual, they always understood it in a deep, full-body way. They would exhale a breathy sigh, a mix of being jealous and happy for me, impressed that I could do something as minor as sit at the bar at a restaurant once a week and put food in my face.

It amazed me how much I came to appreciate the mere act of eating in a restaurant in the middle of the day, and the tremendous pleasure in these otherwise mundane meals. I took them very seriously, and if I missed one for whatever reason—a doctor's appointment, hers or mine, for instance—I would be bitterly wounded by the loss. I would feel the lack all through the following week, like a piece of myself had been stolen, like a debt was being accumulated.

(Even as I write this, I can hear those familiar voices of derision, the ones that will say "if you were going to complain about a loss of freedom maybe you shouldn't have had a child in the first place" and "you knew what you signed up for." As I write this, I am conscious of that dreaded label of "bad mother," the one so easily smacked on those who simply dare to say it's hard, that they don't love it every waking moment, that they just want to eat a meal at a restaurant alone from time to time. I can hear the voices because every mother can hear the voices—they are with her every time she takes a morsel of something—care, joy, time—for herself.)

Occasionally the lunch crowd would look sidelong at me while I ate and drank alone, perhaps out of pity, perhaps simply wondering what my story was. The staring didn't bother me so much—certainly not as it did before my daughter was born. I remember during one of the many phone calls to my mother during that tumultuous time, she expressed deep concern about these outings, as if the very idea of me eating and drinking alone was completely horrifying to her. (The few times I was able to go to the movies alone post-baby upset her even more.)

"I would never do that," she said to me, almost disdainfully.

I idly wonder why she *would never*. Is it because she simply doesn't crave the feeling of being alone with the same intensity as I do, every moment of my day otherwise concerned with the care and feeding and increasingly complex nap schedule of a tiny person? Or is it deeper than that—more *generational* than that? Is the simple yet radical image of dining alone indicative of an individualism that has been denied to her? To her the idea of alone meant only loneliness, when it could, in fact, mean so much more. After all, the very idea that mothers could openly want to be away from their children, that they could be allowed to want a break, even for an afternoon, is a relatively new one.

The long arm of "mom guilt" did follow me into those solo days, but I swatted it away, the cultivation of exquisite solitude becoming my mission. I didn't want company. I didn't want conversation. I wanted quiet, or to simply borrow other people's noise. Generally, I would sit at the bar rather than at a table, always bringing a book or a piece of "work" to build a barrier between me and anyone who felt like they could approach.

Alone, I would listen to the exchanges of the people around me while using the pages of my book to appear like I wasn't. Freelancers pounding away at keyboards, taking calls in their headphones. Colleagues enjoying a leisurely lunch before returning to the office, gossiping about co-workers and complaining about bosses. Young, beautiful, well-put-together women delighting in each other's company, the idea of babies far from their thoughts.

And then there were the loud, bombastic men in very important meetings, with their very important opinions and deadlines and opportunities. Familiar men, exactly the kind who had promised me things in my career and my life—publication, columns, deals, extra dollars, even love—and had never come through. The kind of men who made me feel like I should be grateful for what scraps I had been given. The kind of men who no longer appeared in that eerily quiet email account now that I was a mother.

I listened and I realized I didn't miss them at all. The conversations or the men.

When I was pregnant, one thoughtful mom I know told me that in the quieter moments of new motherhood, she repeated the phrase "I am free" to herself over and over again.

It was, she said, a tactic to remind herself, if only for a few seconds, that the intensity of the burden and connection (both physical and emotional) she had with her child was a choice she made every day, however impossible that choice seemed. It was a way to remind herself that her body was still her own despite how much it had been overtaken and transformed, that she was more than what she sacrificed, more than what she had given up.

That impulse to affirm freedom was one I didn't understand at the time but clung to desperately as my own new motherhood unfolded—this fundamental idea that I still had autonomy and a sense of self amid all the dramatic forgetting, all this evidence to the contrary, all this crying in train stations about what had been left behind. In those early days, freedom so often feels like it has been violently stripped from you. On the other side of this intense connection between mother and child is the feeling of being trapped in a cage of your own making.

Despite my rejection of those early warnings that postpartum I would feel personally and professionally unmoored, I am now wholly aware that all the things that once structured and buoyed my life slipped away from me in that first year of my daughter's life. There were no deadlines to be met or meetings to attend or emails to be sent. Events—whether for business or pleasure—were planned so ridiculously far in advance that nothing was ever spontaneous.

Something as simple as a nap—or worse, a missed nap—had the potential to derail an entire day. But not being malleable spelled inevitable screaming doom.

It remains unclear to me even now whether or not motherhood severed me from the things I once cared about, or if it instead took away my capacity to care about those things at all. I was once an adult doing adult world things, and then I was managing that ridiculously regimented nap schedule, signing up for baby sign language classes, and considering the pros and cons of store-bought or homemade baby food. There was simply no room for even an awareness of high-profile book events, buzzy movie premieres, or who was going to make it to the postseason that year.

There was, however, an unexpected shiny side to that otherwise dull new coin: the smallest moments became so much sweeter, no longer taken for granted. A cold beer sipped in a patch of patio sunlight. A bike ride alone on the Railpath. A walk without a destination. The entirety of an episode of television watched without diversion.

A midday lunch alone.

The baseball games I could no longer attend played on low volume and flickered brightly in the quiet dark of those unmoored early days of motherhood, giving me a fixed thing to look at when everything else seemed chaos.

Sometimes my daughter would let me watch seven innings, sometimes she would interrupt, needing something immediately, sometimes she would make me abandon the game altogether, but this thing that got me through so much would always hum along in the background of my life, marking those loose, early, forgotten moments with its beautiful scheduled consistency. Marking the deepest nights like a lighthouse.

I think in some ways, despite how long I yearned for the word to be one I could claim, I was so terrified of being smothered by the weighted moniker of "mother" that I actively denied and didn't safeguard myself against the possibility. I have since learned that comfort can come from accepting the reality of change and celebrating all the possibilities that accompany it. For me that became the beautiful—if painful—paradox of motherhood: the experience took me further and further away from the person I thought I wanted to be and, in the process, somehow taught me more about myself than I ever thought possible.

In all that forgetting, I seemed to remember. In losing my footing, I felt grounded.

And with all the generous gentle warnings I received, it seems only fair to deliver my own: there is no doubt that a new baby will consume you near entirely. The funny thing is, you won't even really resist. After she's born you will all but totally disappear into that delicate world of two, and you will (very sleepily) say thank you. It will be private and perfect, and you will be grateful for it—the exhaustion, the crying, the bodily fluids and all. And as your life shrinks into its tiniest moving parts, as you are forgetting and being forgotten, you will revel in the simplicity of basic needs filled, of time (and sleep) becoming meaningless, of all those days of being totally exhausted but accomplishing so little, of simply keeping a new life happy and alive.

While all this is happening, you will indeed start to fade from view—both that of others and that of your old self—and again you won't exactly protest. People will stop calling, stop offering that generous shiny newborn help, and that'll be okay too. You will have to remind yourself of your freedom. It will definitely be hard, and sometimes it will hurt a great deal to be severed from what you're used to, but at the end of every sentence you'll say, "I'm just so lucky."

And yes, sure, you'll feel very lucky but you'll also sometimes feel lost, both deliberately and unintentionally forgotten, needing to be unearthed between one line and the next. You'll need to be pried open from all the paragraphs of your life not written. You'll need a small blinking light in the distance to help you remember, a lighthouse to keep you tethered to your sense of self, however evolving it may be. You'll need old markers to chain yourself to, to prevent you from entirely floating away. You'll need a map, a trail of bread crumbs, a ribbon tied around a tree on the overgrown path.

You will need to find the old that fits in with the new—a familiar light to guide you back.

Acts of Nourishment

About a decade ago, after a lifetime of barely muddling my way through the kitchen, I finally learned how to cook.

To do this I ordered a weekly box of produce and embarked on my own crash course in culinary acuity. Although the delivery company gave me the option of curating what fruits and vegetables came to my door, as a personal challenge I opted to work with whatever default surprise they sent my way every Friday evening.

When the box arrived it always smelled alive. Red kale and garlic scapes. Firm shiitake mushrooms and new potatoes coated in dark earth. Juicy heirloom tomatoes and fat, fragrant spring onions. Mangoes, peaches, nectarines, and kiwis, all sweet and sticky.

It was amazing that I had made it so far into adulthood incapable of making myself or anyone else a decent meal. My mother is skilled in the kitchen but never taught me how to cook. I assume this is because she liked to exert control over her immaculate domestic domain, a place where a glass or pot was never left out for more than a moment, where the sink was always bleach clean. As far as I can tell, my father has never made a meal in the close to fifty years they've been married, but he has certainly eaten well, thanks to my mother's typical northern British menu—stews, sausages, Yorkshire pudding, ploughman's lunch, shepherd's pie.

Being excluded from the kitchen was about keeping it pristine, but I also think there was a part of my mother that didn't want her daughter to find herself stuck there. It was a noble intention from a woman who stayed home after I was born and spent much of her life nourishing others. It also meant that when I moved away at nineteen, I ordered takeout and microwaved bean burritos more nights a week than not, making myself cereal for dinner and cooking things like "pasta in mayonnaise."

When I eventually became pregnant with my daughter, after that first trimester bout of severe nausea had finally passed, I spent a large portion of my day in our kitchen, shifting my focus from cooking to baking. Between my writing deadlines and prenatal appointments, I churned out daily batches of baked goods intended to satisfy intense and relentless cravings for all things sweet and buttery. Frosted cakes and fruit loaves littered our limited counter space, my husband gaining a good twenty pounds by my delivery date thanks to my (or rather the baby's) intense sweet tooth.

At the time, I dismissed the maternal stereotype inherent in pulling a dozen freshly baked cookies from the oven with a pair of flower-printed oven mitts, but it's hard not to view that time as me gleefully trying on a role that infertility suggested would be denied to me. Perhaps I was seeing if I could actually perform the storied part of perfect mother, carefully grating lemon rind into a bowl of shortbread dough, whipping up an airy vanilla buttercream for a batch of birthday cupcakes.

Later, in an attempt to nurture my daughter's own interests in cooking, I bought her a play kitchen for her second birthday. It was an unwieldy moulded-plastic thing featuring a replica sink and stove, with a cupboard to store its charmingly tiny cups and dishes. She took to it immediately, and a close friend joked that I shouldn't be imposing domestic duties on her at such an early age. I laughed at the time, but whenever she would retreat to her little fridge and oven to make us an imaginary meal, pulling a stuffed watermelon slice from its plastic bin or cutting neon-green yarn into piles of spaghetti, I would think about that fraught relationship, that delicate line between prescribed duty and reclaimed pleasure.

The weekly produce delivery was a soothing experiment in imposed limitations, a place where I could prove I wasn't helpless, that I was capable of building something with only what I'd been given. While the associations made between food and control are almost always negative—and certainly ones I have been susceptible to throughout my life: calorie counting, crash diets, extreme fasts, disordered eating—this new sacred weekly ritual belied that, and freed me from my own past use of food (or lack of it) as punishment.

Like many women my age, I flirted with disordered eating as a teen in the 1990s and a young adult into the early 2010s. Starvation was my chosen method of control, with the occasional purge not out of the question. My hatred of and need to punish my body were the result of the usual suspects: the media, the hyper diet-conscious adults around me (and their unsolicited commentary), the pressure of my peers, mistreatment by the boys and later men in my life. I discovered I had a gift for overcoming my hunger, for erasing my own desire and need. Food, or rather the restriction of it, offered a way to regain power, however damaging that reclamation proved to be.

The produce box and the weekly surprises it held offered a new kind of power entirely—one that nurtured rather than punished, that celebrated rather than shamed. Learning to put together the pieces of a truly delicious meal helped me fall in love with feasting after a long, fraught relationship with sustenance.

Of the many anxieties I had about bringing another person into the world, ensuring her own enduring love of food was pretty high on the list. Even while I was still breastfeeding, I read countless books about how to build good associations with eating for children, absorbing dictums like serving dessert at the same time as vegetables; never demanding a cleared plate or referring to any particular food as "good" or "bad"; never descending into negative talk about bodies, my own or anyone else's. Still, despite my in-depth research and carefully employed techniques, like a vast majority of children, mine inevitably grew into an incredibly "picky" eater.

With a preference for the food group "beige," my daughter's less-than-expansive palate certainly did not include any creations via the contents of the weekly produce delivery box. She had a strong start with food experimentation as a baby and toddler, but by the time she entered kindergarten, her preferences had narrowed to a list that included little more than frozen chicken fingers, French fries, Eggo waffles, and peanut butter sandwiches (no jam, thank you very much). If we ordered a cheese pizza in a restaurant, we'd need reassurance that there was "no green" on it, lest we have to pick off every tiny stray flake of basil or oregano by hand before she'd even look at it. Ordering her a burger would prompt my husband to make a dramatic arm gesture, clarifying that there was to be nothing on it.

"Not even ketchup?" the server would ask.

"Nothing."

Of course this development was uncomfortable for someone who had a history of restriction, who fought very hard to unlearn limiting meals, who had tried to nurture an environment where food was a joy to be savoured not simply something unboxed, tossed on a sheet pan, and baked at 400°F for eighteen minutes.

The prescribed rules around reforming picky eaters are plentiful but can often be impractical (if not impossible). *Don't let children snack too much during the day. Don't give up on repeatedly introducing a variety of new foods. Don't stray from routine. Don't cater to your child's fussy whims. Don't blame yourself.* But the thing I missed while fretting over what my daughter was or wasn't willing to try was that my hovering obsession became its own problem. Just like being anxious about her inheriting my tendency toward anxiety wouldn't keep worries at bay, pressuring her to eat asparagus wasn't going to make her fall deeply in love with vegetables. Introducing shame and condemnation, however unintentionally, would never encourage the kind of culinary experimentation I now so deeply believed in.

For all my obsessing about my daughter's healthy relationship with food, I forgot she needed the freedom to develop *her own* relationship with food, one that would grow and evolve with time, a relationship that was positive precisely because she had come to it on her own terms, not had it forced upon her by me or anyone else. My job was to guide her and make room for new discoveries—the joy of strawberry ice cream in a cone on a hot summer day, the stickiness of watermelon slices on her fingers after running through a sprinkler, some browning bananas turned into bread warm from the oven, a giant salted pretzel at a baseball game demanding a lemonade chaser with extra ice.

Asparagus—despite being so delicious drenched in butter—could wait.

One Sunday evening in July 2020, I went into the kitchen and pulled out a recipe for puttanesca sauce with roasted eggplant, a dish I had been thinking about preparing for over a week. A deeply satisfying (and wonderfully forgiving) meal to make, the ingredients suggest decadence but are not hard to find—a can of whole tomatoes, an eggplant, anchovies, red wine, dried red chilies, capers, shallots, a cup of Kalamata olives.

Planning meals gave me something to look forward to during the pandemic, a time when it was hard to find anything to look forward to. The connection between food and the realities of lockdown life became obvious as soon as pictures of homemade sourdough loaves were being posted on social media. Many of us found ourselves cooking, baking, sipping, and savouring our way through the endless mundane horror of isolation, embracing food as familiar and much-needed comfort, centring on celebration and creativity, and as a way of wrestling back some much-needed normalcy. For the anxious among us, food became an arena of mastery—a place to plan and execute, to prove that questions could be answered, that problems could be solved.

Even though the kitchen has long been a site of enormous domestic inequality, and is oft-dismissed for mostly gendered reasons, in times of loss and disarray it has the potential to be a deeply grounding and healing place. While submerged in pandemic life, cooking became a surprising way to assert my sense of self when feeling otherwise lost.

The retreat to the kitchen didn't have to be a retreat at all. I could make something real and beautiful and fulfilling on my own terms. I could finally feel in control when everything else felt so completely out of control. After years of mentally preparing for the worst, the worst was here—and despite what I had long believed about myself, I was actually skilled at making it tolerable, if only because I could pull together an incredible plate of pasta.

A good friend of mine—also the mother of a then toddler-aged daughter—joked that the trials of maternity leave had uniquely trained us for the isolation of COVID-19.

"In a lot of ways, it's the same," she said. "Basically, you stay home ninety-nine per cent of the time, and on the rare occasion you go out, you bring a litre of hand sanitizer with you."

Her comment came from a place of much-needed levity, but it wasn't the first time I had heard an exhausted mom say that lockdown felt like some terrible version of new motherhood writ large: sleep deprivation, loneliness, and confusion but without the benefits and structure of park hangouts, coffee dates, and library song circles.

When the pandemic forced us inside a month after my daughter turned two, I started recovering those travel-sized bottles of hand sanitizer from the pockets of my jackets and bags, leftover relics from those anxious early days. Maternity leave was a different kind of sudden and overwhelming shift, but the core coping skills I gained in my postpartum crash course felt oddly applicable in this new, terrible moment: acceptance, being present, and the realization that the only constant is change.

As exhausting and frustrating as children can admittedly be—especially in closed quarters—the cliché remains true: they are often our best teachers. In times of strife, they have this uncanny ability to provide much-needed perspective, even when they are being entirely irrational. They are particularly good at reminding us that nothing will last forever. Every sleep regression, every erupting tooth, every inexplicable behaviour is simply a phase to endure, a shifting goalpost, something you have to and will get through despite how entrenched the moment feels. The worries I had about my daughter when she was a newborn and then a one- and a two-year-old are now so far away as to be irrelevant. Even the worries I had about her last week have already morphed into brand-new ones. It's that transience of concern that makes parenting so heartbreakingly beautiful—immense change happens while time clips by at a lightning pace.

That also makes the various highs and lows of parenthood so hard (if not impossible) to accurately document. Just like I tried to memorize my daughter's face in those first moments I held her after she was born, I often found myself haplessly trying to get the lessons she imparted down on the page. When I think back on that conversation I had with my professor friend at the university so long ago, perhaps the most pressing question of writing about motherhood is not "who would even care" but rather "how could you even articulate it"? The years I've worked on this book have been steeped not only in obscuring emotion but also in delights and devastations that have evolved and changed so much and so quickly. It's like trying to capture a buzzing fly that's gotten in through an open screen door. Each milestone brings new priorities, new reasons to rhapsodize and lament, new amazements and humblings to soak up. Something that mere months ago felt like a meaningful observation to share is pretty much obsolete now.

What does seem to endure through every phase is the oft-repeated idea of the "resilience of children," and it offered a good model given what the pandemic asked of us. Yes, my daughter wanted to see her friends just like I did. She missed the zoo, the swings at the park, and picking out picture books at the library. But at home she also found great pleasure in methodically peeling the labels off crayons, putting fifty pennies in a jar, or having the same book read to her twenty-seven times. These days, she can find joy in building an intricate play structure from a pile of discarded delivery boxes, writing a dozen-page fully illustrated story about a family pet, or inventing an interpretative dance routine to her latest Top 40 obsession. Spending long stretches of time with her when she was a baby, during the pandemic, and now, sometimes feels like a master class in being present in and satisfied with the limited moment.

It turns out becoming a mother meant dramatically relearning not only how to approach life but also the very pace of that approach. I had to actively cultivate patience and become okay with staying in one place for long stretches of time, day after day after day. I had to embrace simplicity, stillness, and quiet, and understand the art of taking things in rather than frantically "doing" all the time. I had to reassess not only what was valuable and meaningful in life but also what gave *me* value and meaning—not, as I previously thought, what I produced and what other people applauded, but how I lived and how I loved.

In so many situations, acceptance is the key to endurance. Embracing imperfection and bending with change, however uncomfortable, is better than breaking because of your own rigidity. Recognizing that something is but won't always be is exactly what cultivates a good life.

It's true I often woke up in the morning and felt that pang of disappointment: yet another day of this monotony, this feeling of being trapped, this fear and uncertainty. But I mustered the strength to try to find tiny lights of hope and places of solace where I could, tried to unearth ways of dealing the same way I unearthed all those little bottles of hand sanitizer.

During our first pandemic summer, my two-year-old daughter took to standing on a stepstool at the kitchen island so she could "help" with the cooking.

I would provide her with whatever random ingredients were available in the pantry that we could reasonably spare to allow her to make a mess. She'd carefully measure flour or shake baking soda into her favourite silver mixing bowl, proudly proclaiming that she was making pancakes, cookies, or cake. She'd create mysterious—and yes, sometimes wholly disgusting—concoctions in that adorable way children do when they're experimenting in the kitchen for the first time.

In isolation, this kind of playing pretend was an obvious reprieve. It was a way for an exhausted and overwhelmed working mother to fill a forty-five-minute block of time when, without daycare or babysitters or kindly grandparent visits, parenting seemed to stretch into oblivion. But it was also an early way to nurture the deep satisfaction that cooking has the potential to bring, to show my daughter that food could be so much more than just inconvenient necessity—or potential enemy. It could be attention, connection, and love during a time when her circle—our circle—was so painfully small. And unlike the kitchen in the home I grew up in—the one I was so often, for better or worse, excluded from—what happened here didn't always have to be perfect. It could be deliberately messy—*we* could be deliberately messy.

"Cooking, for me now, is an opportunity for unstructured play—which very well may be why I am so opposed to using recipes," writes Chelene Knight in her book *Let it Go: Free Yourself from Old Beliefs and Find a New Path to Joy*. "I love the idea that I can create something without rules and that making mistakes is part of the process. I can assess and reassess what works and what doesn't. The more I fell into this unstructured play, the more cooking became an even bigger part of my joy, and it helped me deduce that although food was problematic when I was younger, it didn't have to stay that way."

Far from imposing domestic duties on my daughter at such an early age, our shared kitchen experiments—however humble and inedible—came to feel like a kind of reclamation.

Despite the fact that I mostly avoided the news to maintain my sanity during lockdown—alloting myself only ten minutes a day—I couldn't avoid the ubiquitous reports that women overall were experiencing a more significant loss of employment hours and income than men. According to the Canadian Women's Foundation, women accounted for sixty-three per cent of the jobs lost as of March 2020, and a national poll rolled out in September of that year indicated that a full one-third of women in Canada considered leaving their jobs entirely "to better manage childcare and other domestic work." The most chilling stat that made the rounds was that women's participation in the labour force was down to its lowest level in three decades—two pandemic months had wiped out thirty-five years of progress.

By the third month of isolation, I personally knew of so many parents who, in lieu of any reliable childcare, had to opt out of the work they loved. A grant writer, a textile designer, a non-profit director, a medical copywriter. By necessity and not by choice, many of my friends suddenly became stay-at-home mothers. Their lower paycheques (already dictated by the gender pay gap) meant that they be the ones to step away and fill the childcare void that everyone just assumed they would fill, without any real knowledge of how vast that void was eventually going to be. And while the government repeatedly told us that daycare was available, mine and so many others simply didn't have the necessary funding to open under the new pandemic guidelines.

With my suddenly severely truncated workdays, I took on small jobs here and there, walking a fine, impossible line between fear of overwhelm and fear of not having enough money to pay the bills. When work would sporadically come I would rejoice, but then anxiously wonder when I would find the uninterrupted time to complete it while also trying to run a sort of subpar at-home preschool—an hour of writing wedged between leading toddler music class and that day's session of gluing eyes on painted rocks, or in the obscenely early window of darkness before my daughter would wake up.

After eighteen months of maternity leave, I had five months of a childcare-supported attempt at full-time work—five months of trying to rebuild my career—before the pandemic hit us and I was at the kitchen island doing crafts most of my days. My personal pandemic story, though not ideal, is certainly not the worst and, oddly, maybe even had its own distinct benefits. I remain grateful my daughter wasn't old enough to really know what was going on or what she was missing out on, grateful she wasn't young enough that my experience of birth and new motherhood was coupled with forced isolation.

In my new kitchen-island reality, I once again had to say no to opportunities, exclude myself because of my ever-present child. No morning radio spots, no quick-turnaround print deadlines, nothing that necessitated any accommodation. Baseball, subject matter I had written about for eight years, was not even happening, and former colleagues were laid off in droves. A Mother's Day piece I devoted hours and hours to while my daughter was still in her now-closed daycare—ironically a piece about new motherhood and subsequently shifting identity—was deemed unsuitable because it was "not really appropriate right now given everything that's going on." The magazine editor rightly assumed there wouldn't be much interest in that kind of heady exploration when we were all in basic survival mode.

"How about we shelve it for the time being?" she wrote via email, my anticipated invoice evaporating into the ether.

I would stand at that kitchen island with my daughter and long to get back to the book I was supposedly writing, this book that I thought would be about the struggle of new motherhood, about the loss of identity that accompanies that shift, but would eventually really be about healing.

The pandemic made many of us feel like our dreams, both large and small, were dying. The plans we so carefully set, the things that defined us daily, all but evaporated, and while we would recover some in time, many parts drifted so far away we struggled to salvage them at all.

Sometimes my brain would follow a train of thought into deep jealousy—of those whose lives seemed to continue on normally, whose plans weren't derailed, whose dreams weren't dashed. People who didn't lose their jobs and instead seemed to excel in isolation, using the time to finish a novel, take up a fun new hobby, generally self-improve, and not fall into total burnout or despair. (I had no proof of this, again only what their social media accounts suggested.) Other times my brain would go to a place of pure rage—at people who wouldn't wear masks, who had a blatant disregard for others, whose general selfishness superseded care and community. (I had proof of this on the sidewalks and in the park, dodging those who didn't make space, watching others gather in large, festive groups.)

How dare they, I would think to myself, my daughter hundreds of days out from playing with another child.

But more than anything I would worry about her. I would worry in a way that felt more solid and genuine than the amorphous buzz of postpartum anxiety or my earlier anxiety diagnosis. It reached far beyond the day-to-day of the pandemic—about what she would remember and what she would forget, about who she would become and what she would have to overcome. About whether or not she would be safe.

And when that worry got too great, when I felt like my entire sense of self was being whittled away by a genuine lack of choices, by an uncertain future, I would choose to temporarily lose myself in the making of an elaborate meal.

For years, my life felt like it was in stasis, like it was unintentionally suspended in the "temporary."

First, I was infertile, a time when I was always waiting for something—someone—else to begin. Then I was finally pregnant, which is a very specific temporary state, one with a scheduled end. Then, as a new mother I was on maternity leave, a time when, perhaps paradoxically, it feels like everything is on hold despite the flurry of activity. Then just when things felt ready to "begin" again for me, the pandemic arrived, putting not just my life but all our lives on truly bizarre hold, together yearning for the end we were promised.

This reality does not make me special, but it does make me confused.

What identity can I claim now? Who am I supposed to be when I am so far away from who I was before this all began? What can I do to make things better? What new stories can I tell myself about myself?

An eggplant salted and peppered, roasted to sweetness. Simmering tomato passata flaked with dried red chilies. Fresh parsley pulled from the garden and roughly chopped. The roar of boiling salted water.

There have been taco nights, and pizza nights, and a few ice-cream-for-dinner nights. I've assembled dozens of comforting canned-soup casseroles, epic four-hour velvety stews from scratch, and one rather adorable rainbow birthday cake for a stuffed dog named Bean. I have made a beloved friend's favourite rhubarb crumble bars, Julia Child's beef bourguignon, cacio e pepe, Rice Krispie squares, and my mother's famous cheese, onion, and potato pie.

(I get requests for my mother's recipe all the time. It's no more complicated than boiling some peeled potatoes, combining them with a splash of milk, a pat of butter, and a whole chopped raw onion, and grating in a half brick of sharp cheese—in my opinion Red Leicester works best. Mash it up, fill your pie shell, and bake at 350°F for about forty minutes. Enjoy, but with the knowledge that for some inexplicable reason both yours and mine will never be as good as my mother's version.)

Some of the dishes I've made have been hilarious failures that remind me of those early days with the produce box when I first started learning—the pancakes missing an egg, the dumplings that fell apart, the bread that resembled an actual brick. Others have offered surprising success—cauliflower mint rice, roasted radishes in coarse salt and lemon, a perfect medium-rare steak butter-basted on the barbecue. Some things I made for reasons of economy, or mastery, or pure affection—to see that wilted vegetable used up, to see a sad leftover put to inventive use, to see the people I love taken care of. Others I made to cultivate patience and acceptance, a love of small rituals, little communions, tiny pleasures.

In 1942, author M.F.K. Fisher released *How to Cook a Wolf*—a book I recalled from a long-ago university food literature class and repurchased during the early pandemic. In this part cookbook, part essay collection, part font of wisdom, Fisher aims to inspire courage and creativity in the kitchen during a time of intense anxiety, unfathomable uncertainty, and the reality of wartime food shortages.

"I believe that one of the most dignified ways we are capable of, to assert and then reassert our dignity in the face of poverty and war's fears and pains, is to nourish ourselves with all possible skill, delicacy, and ever increasing enjoyment," she wrote. "And with our gastronomical growth will come, inevitably, knowledge and perception of a hundred other things, but mainly of ourselves. Then Fate, even tangled as it is with cold wars as well as hot, cannot harm us."

Food is, of course, nourishing and life-giving—even life-saving. But I also went to enough socially distanced neighbourhood park and Zoom dinners to know that food brings us together even when we're asked to be physically apart. By putting so much care into the preparation of a meal, by allowing food to lend structure, and by making it the focal point of our days, eating has the potential to become a temporary reprieve from the uncertainty that is everywhere. (An evolved position on food I'm very proud of, so far away from my teenage days where self-imposed starvation seemed to be the logical solution to chaos.)

The world may be falling apart, but you can pull together a simple and satisfying sauce for your pasta. You can break bread with the people you want to keep safe. You can leave a meal on the porch of a person you can't share a table with. You can swap recipes, and drop off coveted ingredients, and make a loved one feel loved. (A neighbour leaving a single, much-needed egg in my mailbox, tenderly wrapped in a delicate scarf, is a particularly fond memory.) You can share a feast with your community and find the space for yourself when your sense of self feels stolen. Everything can feel wrong, but we can still conjure gratitude, pleasure, and plenty. We can still enjoy a meal.

Then Fate cannot harm us.

I made meals to make sure nothing was wasted in a time where things felt taken from us. I made meals to conjure strength, gratitude, and plenty, when all three felt fleeting. I made meals to find myself, and that delicate line between duty and pleasure.

Writing After Her

When the writing finally returned to me, it did so in a messy wave of need.

About four months after my daughter was born, I started to wake up in the middle of the night not because it was time for a feeding, but because I had an incredible drive to put things down on paper. I needed to get some random, mostly unformed thought documented, scrawled haphazardly on whatever surface was available at the time, the writing lit only by the dim glow of street lamps through my window.

The bedroom where my daughter, husband, and I slept became littered with these frenzied notations, scribbled on receipts and napkins, defacing the inside covers of my books. Many of them were near illegible, written blind in the dark while everyone else slept. Others ended up in the notes section of my phone, next to lists of baby things to do or buy or organize, my innermost thoughts becoming largely absurd thanks to the tyranny of autofill. When morning came, I would translate and decipher every line, diligently transcribing each into what had been a long-empty notebook, waiting in a box by the bed.

You need a map—a trail of bread crumbs, one note read. *A ribbon tied around a tree on the overgrown path. A North Star to guide you back to yourself.*

I would run my fingers over the messy scrawl, hoping that maybe this particular line or that particular line was the one that would rescue me from the ongoing baby-related writing drought, the line that would finally bring me back to myself.

Before I became a mother, I had been arrogant enough to proclaim writer's block didn't exist. Writing was work, not magic, and not being able to do it simply suggested a lack of interest or motivation. But then I had my baby and my mind simply wouldn't work the way it did before. It didn't ruminate on big ideas, form acidic opinions, or leap from one word to the other in a graceful arc. Instead it stumbled along haplessly, dealing with whatever immediate task was at hand and drunk on my devotion to my daughter, exhausted and preoccupied, incapable of any further creation.

The fog that everyone promised descended.

Every word that did manage to make it to the page was saturated with doubt. Of course, all writers mistrust the quality of their work from day to day, but this was far more concerning, far more debilitating. This was a new, insidious kind of uncertainty. After decades of knowing clearly that writing was the thing I was meant to do, after years of taking risks and contorting my life to make this my vocation, I wondered if I should even bother writing at all.

Who will care? the doubt called out. *Do* I *even care anymore?*

New motherhood meant feeling incapable of properly caring for this inexplicable creature in my arms, and that feeling of being incapable bled into other arenas of my life where I had once been able to manage. People—writers and mothers I admired—had quietly and cautiously warned me this might happen. They told me that I would be amazed at how little I could do and how much of my self would be lost, but thanks to my proven history of ambition and manic productivity, my well-established use of overwork as a salve, I assumed my particular postpartum situation would be different. I assumed that *I was different*.

I remember at one point, hugely pregnant, asking my agent, a seasoned mother of two herself, if she thought I would be able to judge a literary magazine's non-fiction contest three months postpartum. I remember the exact weight and length of her pause, the way she slowly, carefully, and very kindly chose her words.

"Well, that depends."

Like many, she gently suggested I shouldn't take on too many things. That I should instead take it easy and take my time. I didn't believe them and I didn't heed their advice. I took on too many things and regretted all the things I took on.

I was so sure I would prove something with my output—but who I needed to prove that to was unclear. Against all odds, I would be the one poised to perfectly answer that awful yet all-too-common gendered question: "How are you so prolific with so much on your plate?" I thought that my inherent workaholic nature would make it possible for me to write a novel and a memoir and countless book reviews and personal essays and spontaneous hot takes while on maternity leave. (It didn't.) I imagined my mind would be quick and my analysis profound, whipping together something laudable while my baby reliably napped. (It wasn't.)

What I did not assume was how soon I would come to reject that ethos of workaholism that had long buoyed me through my anxiety and my grief, and how immediately I would feel my writing—and my self—disappear as a result.

It's not an exaggeration to say that the year before my daughter was born, I was probably the best version of my professional self I had ever been. So many years after that first panic attack, I felt well enough to thrive, my worry no longer following me like a dark cloud of personal sabotage, my productivity subsequently soaring.

I had done years of work on myself to get to that point—so many hours of so many different kinds of therapy to finally come to a place where I wasn't afraid of being alive and out there. I had been able to quit my office job and take the leap into full-time writing. I was generating story ideas, pitching them near constantly, writing for multiple venues, and, despite the stress, generally enjoying what I was doing. I had published a bestselling book. I had spent time in the Blue Jays spring training locker room with my tape recorder, achieving what I had dreamed of for so long. After fighting so hard, I felt heard and seen, and had found a version of success that seemed to satiate me.

I felt like a great deal of my hard work had been validated by external forces, but what felt more important was the fact that I liked what I was producing. The writing felt authentic. It felt real. It felt like I had found myself. I felt like I knew what I was doing.

Having a baby felt like the opposite of that. There was no one to tell me I was doing a good job at this thing, and every day I felt like I was constantly floundering.

By the time I found out I was pregnant with my daughter in the spring of 2017, my workaholic stint had helped me secure a monthly baseball column and the media credentials to go with it. I had my dream job and had finally fulfilled my dream of starting a family.

But from the very beginning, the work I both loved and hated, the work that exhausted but had also come to define me, refused to accommodate my pregnancy. The first trimester involved fighting the urge to vomit while being interviewed about the aforementioned book at public events, on the radio, and on television. A stint of promotional spots in Calgary necessitated that I lift the shroud of early pregnancy secrecy and tell the publicist who was managing my schedule that I was seven weeks along, allowing her to manage (and explain away) my near-constant need to find a discreet place to puke.

I was so grateful to have media access to the ballpark, but it turned out it was impossible for me to even go to the stadium. I could barely stay up past 8 p.m. thanks to extreme tiredness, and when I did manage to drag myself to an evening game, the smell of beer, popcorn, and hotdogs made my stomach lurch. I lied to my editor and claimed I was more interested in thoughtful human-interest stories and baseball book reviews than recaps or post-game interviews, landing me in publishers' offices interviewing memoir-writing retired athletes instead of being close to the action. (Though I did appreciate the post-interview parenting advice from P.K. Subban's author-dad.)

That baseball stadium–induced nausea is the kind of ironic, cosmic joke you might find in a Hollywood mom-com, but it was emblematic of something much less funny. The mother I had so longed to be was already in conflict with the person I had ambitiously built in her absence.

Even in those early days of pregnancy, as much as I scrambled to make things work, deep inside I knew this part of my career—what had so long defined me and my worth—would be over. And when childbirth pulled me even further away, I had to reflect on what I wanted to be when I came back to a world that I felt had mostly forgotten my existence.

Everyone knows that under the umbrella of pregnancy, childbirth, and motherhood are some pervasive ideas about "getting back" to what came before. Of course, the most common and insidious are about the postpartum body and the apparent need for it to return to its pre-baby state as quickly as possible (both unnecessary and impossible, by the way). Celebrity magazines and gossip websites are saturated with photos of famous new moms, with inappropriate body-related comments ranging from "can you believe she's had a baby?" to "can you believe how much she's let herself go?" After I gave birth, so many sponsored posts on my Instagram account were asking me if I longed to look like I did before I did the exhausting work of making a whole other human, and when exactly I was going to start doing stroller workouts and baby-accompanied Pilates to make sure what was reflected back at me in the mirror was acceptable.

This major life change, this monumental spiritual, emotional, and physical shift, is treated like a mere blip, as if someone hit the pause button and I would magically come back to the page as easily as I (should be able to) fit into that old pair of jeans. The applause feels so much louder for women who decide to launch a clothing line or skin care company with a new baby on their hip, so much quieter for the women who (quite rightly) decide to simply rest. The "supermama" is an insidious cultural icon, a woman—usually found in the filtered mists of social media—who is somehow able to raise her well-dressed, adorable children and run her burgeoning (typically mom-centric) business at the same time, all while managing numerous hair and beauty appointments, daily gym visits, date night with her husband, and looking absolutely immaculate.

How does she do it? (The answer is "with lots of money, lots of help, and lots of highlight reels.")

The resources for mothers to emotionally weather this huge change are scarce, especially if you don't have the dollars to procure them. I spent a lot of my early postpartum time immobile and without adult company, meaning social media became my nefarious instructional guide—a poisonous soup of conflicting and often judgmental information that left me floundering. I became convinced that the magical return to what came before could be achieved by simply powering through the hard times and "never giving up," by being a "no excuses mama," or some other grotesque online catchphrase. It didn't occur to me that it could be best achieved via the understanding, care, and support of my community, or by the accommodations of my industry, or by institutionalized health and wellness supports aiming to ease the transition.

After I was discharged from the hospital with perineal stitches, the only professional care I received was a few visits from the doula and the lactation consultant I was fortunate enough to be able to pay for out-of-pocket, that phone call from Toronto Public Health asking if I thought I might have postpartum depression, and the infamous six-week postpartum appointment in which my OBGYN took a brief look at my healing wounds and cleared me to exercise and have sex. The comprehensive schedule of routine medical examinations were reserved for my daughter, but I, her barely mobile shuffling zombie food source, had to get her there with my equally underslept husband by my side. This of course was all compounded by my pervasive postpartum anxiety, which made it seemingly impossible to reach out for—or accept—the community care I so desperately needed at my most vulnerable.

Our culture constantly demands that women fit into systems that don't accommodate them, and the foray into motherhood is no exception. That bald-faced lie that "you can have it all," drilled into us for decades, makes moms believe that no matter how hard the world is beating them down, no matter how much they're struggling without help, they can find happiness, success, and fulfillment, as long as they find *the power within*. I felt this messaging all around me when I was trying to claw my way back to some semblance of a career postpartum, whether from the mom boss influencers algorithmically hurled at me on social media, the woo-woo self-help tomes I found myself turning to out of desperation, or the bootstrap "I did it on my own" mentality of the generation that came before us.

The idea that sheer will is the thing that will set you up for success in early motherhood (or anywhere else, for that matter) is a ridiculous and cruel claim. You're doomed to fail and then told to blame yourself for said failure because "the only thing stopping you is you."

All of this is likely the reason I wrongly assumed I would be able to (and even want to) take my daughter everywhere with me immediately after she was born—literary conferences and publishers' offices and other people's book launches. I assumed I would give readings and talks with her strapped to my body and breastfeed her in the front row of a lecture I desperately wanted to attend. (Instead of conferences, meetings, and lectures, we ended up at Disney on Ice, Sesame Street Live, and a monster truck rally. She didn't attend her first book event until she was five—naturally, the launch of a picture book.)

As I came to understand how difficult it would be to cling to my work connections with a new baby in tow, the eventual transition back to full-time freelance work started to terrify me. No one was calling because I had nothing to say, and who was I if there was no need to listen to me? I felt like I was adrift in an ocean, still emotionally hooked to the things I loved but with no one to reel me back in.

In my increasing postpartum isolation, I developed an unhealthy jealousy when it came to those who were able to go on maternity leave from an office job at a company. Beyond the financial security, a company was required by law to reserve a spot, a place to come back to, offering an opportunity to step outside a given identity for a time and then step right back into it. Of course I know that it's not that easy or simple. Parents in more traditional working environments suffer from a challenging return-to-work identity crisis just like any freelancer, but perhaps that's the point. I was assuming that a different working situation would solve what felt impossible to solve, when really the problems were much bigger than whether I was on payroll or invoicing or even making the decision to stay at home for an undetermined length of time.

The pressure to return to my former self—writer and otherwise—was entirely suffocating. How exactly could I get back to anything if that third-degree tear meant I could barely get out of bed? How exactly would I cover a baseball game or do a reading in a postpartum adult diaper, or with a breastfeeding baby who needed me around the clock, or when my relentless fatigue meant I could barely make it to the end of an event without falling asleep?

How exactly could anything—my body, my career, my values, my sense of self—ever be the same again?

Thanks to the rose-tinted (or perhaps green-eyed) window that is social media, I was keenly aware of what every other writer and mother I knew and didn't know was doing. Even though I fought against this ugly impulse, I was constantly comparing my lot to theirs, taking a complex mental tally. How long did it take them, postpartum, to publish again? How much was their output? How easy was it for them? (Always easier than it was for me, it seemed.)

One beautiful, glossy dark-haired scribe fuelled my insecurity like no other. Beyond the fact that she was effortlessly gorgeous, she seemed to furtively write and edit through pregnancy and postpartum, releasing an acclaimed book around her son's first birthday. To add to my envy, she also seemed to get pregnant effortlessly, posting a glowing picture of herself, swollen with her second child, the same week she announced her latest project.

She became the ethereal, angelic, totally unrealistic marker against which I measured myself and my success, even though I knew I didn't have the full picture of her life. I didn't know what kind of help she had at home, how hard it actually was for her day to day, when and how she wrote. I just knew she was doing so much better than me and that meant I was failing.

I shared this shameful feeling with a friend, also struggling with a tiny baby and wondering how to climb back to herself. I told her that I thought my career was falling apart, diving off the cliff of my daughter's birth, and that I had no idea how I would pull it all back together again given how much had been lost.

"But you look like you're doing so well," she said.

When it came down to it, what I really cared about losing in the wake of new motherhood was time. I hated that nagging feeling that in devoting myself to my daughter I was shelving myself, my life, my work, my own distinct identity. Each pressing, anxious thought I had about her well-being felt like one that was keeping out all those other creative thoughts that were hammering at the door, keeping all those inspired notes from being written in the middle of the night.

What was worse, I hated myself for that creeping, ugly need to simply be alone. How could I possibly desire *freedom,* however temporary, from this person I so long wanted in my life? Didn't longing for that space for myself, however small, make me a bad mother? My deepest need and my deepest guilt were one and the same: I just wanted to shut a door and be assured it wouldn't open again until I opened it. What I didn't want to feel during any time I did manage to spend alone was this terrible creeping urgency, like watching sand through an hourglass slip away. I hated needing to pack every tiny piece of time I had to myself with both productivity and rejuvenation. (Impossible, by the way.) I hated the pressure to return to her having completed a mountain of work and feeling fully restored. (Also impossible.)

Those moments when I resented motherhood, when I only wanted her away from me and finally off my body, were also the ones that preceded missing her with an impossible full-body ache. Ones where instead of working on anything of genuine substance, I simply flipped through pictures of her on my phone.

People kept telling me to give it time, but time passed and nothing even vaguely resembled what came before. I got calls to be on the radio for times that were impossible to accommodate, or writing deadlines that I simply wouldn't be able to meet. After I said no a few times out of newborn-related necessity, the calls and emails ceased completely. Friends, fellow writers, and former colleagues all told me my new sense of irrelevancy was just in my imagination, simply all in my head. But the facts bore out a completely different story: I lost columns and clients and calls for new work.

It turned out if I went easy on myself, I would simply make things harder for myself. The cultural reassurance that I could have it all felt like nothing more than gaslighting.

I've come to understand a less obvious but just as urgent reason writing postpartum is so difficult: *you really don't know who you are*

anymore. To write well you must have a genuine sense of identity, or at least some vague signposts to attempt to figure that out. Who you were fades near completely from view in the months leading up to labour, and then totally evaporates in the screaming moment of birth. You lose yourself, the threads of before slipping away more quickly than you can gather them up and cling to them.

In the physical and emotional aftermath of birth, I simply wasn't as passionate about the things I once cared enough about to document. I didn't have the attention span to finish a movie, was too distracted and tired to stay up to watch an entire baseball game, and couldn't even dream of finishing—let alone giving a thoughtful, critical analysis of—a newly released work of literature. As for any sort of self-reflexive writing? My daughter took up so much room in my psyche, was so close up in my view, that I couldn't fathom writing anything more than her name over and over again.

Things seem to work out much better for those who immediately surrender to that dramatic change: those who happily relish leaving their jobs, who enjoy baby shopping and adorable tiny things, who write saccharine Instagram pregnancy captions like "I love you already" and "can't wait to finally meet you!" But for those of us who cling to what we were before the noun "mother" came stomping in, the transition is much more difficult, as is the eventual letting go.

(The letting go is completely necessary. There is no other way through it.)

The things you love, the things that define you—the pleasure of words on a page, of men in clean white uniforms taking the field on a summer day, of a book read in a single afternoon—they all start to fall away. There is no infatuation left to give away, no room left in the face of this monumental, helpless, immediate need in your lap.

For a time, you are nothing more than the fulfillment of that beautiful need. The rest fades, flickers in the background of survival. It's hard to care about the things you loved before, the things that make you who you are, when you are trying so hard to keep something helpless alive. That is an all-consuming project.

Despite what I had been told and promised, despite what I had assumed, despite what I needed and tried to force—the way we have built modern motherhood doesn't leave a lot of room for anything else at all.

Three things I wish someone had warned me about, without whispers and caveats, without smiles and asterisks:

I wish someone had said, "you have to learn how to be okay with being a new—perhaps unrecognizable—version of yourself."

I wish someone had said, "you have to come to terms with and properly grieve the loss of what came before."

I wish someone had told me that beyond not being able to, I probably wouldn't even want to be doing a public reading with a human being strapped to my body, that instead I would want a nap and to watch an entire episode of television that I picked out and find some sense of autonomy and freedom and quiet and the chance to have a warm cup of coffee alone in a coffee shop on a sunny day.

Before my daughter arrived, I was convinced my worth lay in my bylines, in writing eight-hundred-word pieces for very little money while strangers online called me all sorts of vile names. I thought the insults and threats I commonly found in my inbox were simply the price of success, as was that general feeling of personal and professional exhaustion—constantly hustling and fighting to be heard, growing accustomed to people treating me badly, and feeling badly more days than not.

At home with my baby, I felt that knee-jerk pang of jealousy, yearning for a life that had been lost that I could never get back. As much as I had complained about my past life ad nauseam, as much as it filled me with dread and anxiety and occasionally fear, I missed how alive it made me feel. I missed being known and seen. I missed feeling like I mattered.

It took me a very long time to understand I still mattered—albeit in a very different way.

It took me a long time to understand not only that I mattered to her but also that I mattered to me.

And while I so often found myself writhing and gasping, straining to hold on to the professional stress that had actually been harming me, things that the baby left no room for, it wasn't until I loosened my grip that I understood what was best.

The writing drought ended eventually, of course.

Around the same time my daughter took her first step, I opened that bedside notebook filled with all my messy attempts in the dark to find something I had lost. Behind a closed bedroom door (that wouldn't open again until I wanted it to), I began the process of moving those once frantically scrawled notes into an open Word document and, with some time and patience, transformed that document into a manuscript.

I liked the simple metaphor in those shared first steps, as if we were both venturing out into the world together—me returning, and she for the first time. Apparently, we were both also very late. Through that deceptive online window, I saw so many more diligent, inspired, miraculous mom/writers who completed full manuscripts and wrote countless essays while on maternity leave—about the same number as miraculous babies walking by the end of their first year.

It seemed my daughter liked to take her time in all things in a way I myself could not. She was unfazed by dictated timelines. She couldn't see the point of pushing herself to do something before she was really ready. And while I was irritated by how hard it was (and still is) to get her to do anything quickly, I was also inspired by her thoughtfulness and her patience with herself—even if I myself couldn't adhere to it.

Why didn't I do more? Why couldn't I do more? the doubt asked back then.

Three things that I am saying to you now:

I regret all the time I wasted being angry and jealous and frustrated with myself, thinking I was failing and not doing enough and wishing I could fit my old life into my new one, wondering how I could "get back" to the writer and person I was.

I regret not exploring what words, ideas, and lives were possible under my new circumstances instead of lamenting what had been lost.

I regret not being kinder to myself.

Toward the very end of my maternity leave, just before my daughter was to begin attending daycare, I was given an assignment to cover a hundred-year-old annual baseball tournament in a small cottage community in southwestern Ontario. I hadn't written a magazine piece, let alone one of this size, for more than two years.

I also had never been away from my daughter overnight.

As part of the assignment, I'd have to travel to the cottage community that housed the tournament and stay with a host family who had offered to put me up in their lake house for the evening. The photographer assigned to the piece would give me a lift to the location, almost three hours outside of the city. It was a lengthy car ride with a complete stranger, and because of that, I was very grateful that he was an affable sort, with a gift for both humour and conversation.

The photographer had two small children himself—one a toddler, the other less than a year old. After engaging in the typical small talk about our kids, he shared with me an interesting theory about what he believed happened to creative people when they have children.

The pursuit of any art, he told me as we travelled together on the lonely two-lane highway, was, at its core, to create something in one's own image. The attempt to make something beautiful and meaningful was almost always in the hope of leaving behind a reflection of oneself in the world. In that sense, having a child who has your nose or your laugh is a pretty straightforward way to fulfill that urge. An actual living, breathing version of you could prove an easy way to lose interest in creating essays or photos or paintings.

"It starts to feel pointless," he said. "You're never going to make anything nearly as perfect."

Why bother?

While I don't think it's true that a child is the greatest thing an artist can produce, the photographer's highway musings provided me with an enormous sense of relief. It made me feel a great deal better about the fact that the intensity of that lifelong drive to write had dissolved, that the things I once cared so much about had fallen away, and that I wasn't alone in this upending life shift. It soothed me to know there was a reason I was happy to leave behind what came before, releasing for good what was worth letting go of. It made me feel like there was something new in the future—a different process, a different way of thinking and valuing expression, a different season—if only I was patient and let it come.

That afternoon the photographer and I ate with the family that had generously offered to put us up, gathering in the sun on the cottage's back patio to hungrily feast on hash browns baked in the oven, burgers grilled on the barbecue, and a creamy pasta salad scooped onto paper plates. With my overnight bag slung over my shoulder, I followed the woman who owned the cottage down to their small but pristine one-room lake house, the place where I would spend the night before covering the community ball game in the morning. The room had pine ceilings, and its queen-sized bed was covered with a festive fauna-printed bedspread. A tiny wooden desk sat invitingly under a window that overlooked the water.

"I hope it's okay," she said.

"It's perfect."

That night, before I went to bed, I pulled out my laptop, my notebook, and my pen and laid them out on the surface of the desk where I would write up my notes from the game the following day. Then, alone in that borrowed room with no baby or wave of need to wake me, I slept deeply for the first time in a long time, lulled by the sound of water lapping against the shore.

A Small, Good Life

Almost three months after my daughter was born, I went to a book launch at the city's largest library. Though it may sound ridiculous, I felt very brave doing so—the event was one of my very first postpartum outings alone, and the first time I would see many of my former publishing colleagues since I had disappeared into motherhood. I had looked forward to the launch of my friend's book for weeks, pumped my milk and planned diligently, embracing the rare outing without my very new baby. I had even consulted one of the internet's many mom blogs to find postpartum-friendly jean recommendations, landing on ones that touted stretch for comfort but still made me feel reasonably put together. After weeks and weeks of wearing something in the neighbourhood of pyjamas (or "Ma-jamas," as another writer friend hilariously called them), getting dressed was a spectacular enough feat in itself.

But as soon as I arrived, I felt uncomfortable. My clothes didn't seem appropriate, nor did they feel like they fit me right. My newly acquired jeans too snug over my slowly deflating belly, my striped button-down rumpled, my bra stuffed with breast pads for fear of leaks. Inside that bustling, wide-open space I felt out of place and weirdly far away from everything, even if going to a book launch was something I had done dozens, if not hundreds, of times before. I didn't really know how to make small talk, didn't really know how to talk about anything other than my daughter, didn't remember how to *be an actual person* out in the world.

My friends from the newspaper I freelanced for, from the magazine I had worked at, from the writing community at large: I should have been overjoyed to see them all after being cooped up for the better part of three months. But standing there in those ill-fitting clothes, I was still totally consumed by this tiny world of two I'd left behind at home. I felt like I was desperately boring, floundering at being social, struggling to enjoy myself.

Beyond that I full-body *missed* my daughter. Even though I had wanted to be free for the night—and for many nights before that—all I could think about was her. Another one of the many emotional contradictions I experienced daily.

The beautiful, successful crowd gathered and took their seats, and I opted to lean against a pole at the very back of the room, reluctant to find a place with the rest of them just in case I felt the sudden need to retreat. I checked the time and considered another glass of wine, taking a mental inventory of pumped milk at home in the fridge.

I loved my friend. I wanted to support her new book. This was the kind of environment I had long felt comfortable in. I was supposed to want to be here—and all I really wanted to do was go home.

It's not much of an exaggeration to say that we exist in a poisonously positive culture that constantly discourages us from quitting anything. "Never give up," the personal mantras espouse. "Anything is possible" and "You got this, girl."

So often I have stayed in situations, both personal and professional, that have been actively harming me, all the while clutching tight to those oft-repeated extreme positivity platitudes. If only I worked hard enough, I would think. If only I gave it my all, put in those extra hours, exerted and exerted to the point of exhaustion. If only I was *really* committed, burning myself out in pursuit of my dreams—then I could have everything I always wanted, even if I'm not entirely sure exactly what forces are feeding that want.

Because of these particular internalized beliefs, I have stayed with men who have harmed me, under bosses who have demoralized me, in living and working situations where I was floundering. I have written pieces on impossibly unaccommodating deadlines, about things that were incredibly difficult and exposing, often for incredibly low pay, and occasionally for some not very nice people—pieces that garnered me online abuse with little or no support from the publications for which I wrote them.

In that spirit of "I can do anything" I have put off rest, and care, and healing. I have tried to prove myself worthy by what and how much I can take, by how far I will go—certainly not by how well I can take care of myself.

By doing all this I have learned a pretty nasty truth: the more you endure, the more you will be asked to endure—and motherhood is no exception.

Writing was doing the work I loved for people I sometimes didn't like very much, while motherhood was doing work I sometimes didn't like very much for someone I loved more than anyone else in the world. (You can love your baby, love doing what's best for your baby, and still hate singing "The Wheels on the Bus" in front of strangers, hate blending mountains of steamed sweet potatoes into consumable mash, hate dumping out an overfull diaper pail.) And just like I wasn't allowed to complain to or about the powers that be that signed my cheques, I wasn't allowed to complain about the genuinely challenging labour of motherhood, no matter how monotonous or exhausting it became. Just like I had to sacrifice certain elements of my comfort, privacy, and mental health for my writing career, I had to sacrifice a lot of my dreams and desires for motherhood.

"That's just part of the job," both vocations screamed. "You knew what you were signing up for."

While I was leaning on that concrete pole at the back of the room at the book launch, a former colleague of mine—someone I hadn't seen for many years—snuck over to say hello. It was a few moments before the onstage interview was to officially begin, so we caught up quickly in hushed tones, happily sharing updates.

She'd once been an editor at the magazine I myself had worked at—a magazine that fostered great loyalty but was prone to giving its employees a bad case of burnout—and had gone on mat leave and simply never come back. I admit there had been moments when I wondered *what happened to her*, had been (now, shamefully) confused about why she'd given up such an "important" job and life to do something "less glamorous."

My former colleague, now a mother of two, congratulated me on my own new addition and asked me how it was going. I gave the usual appropriate canned spiel that boiled down to "hard but good" and then, in my big event-related vulnerability, confided how outside of everything I felt in that moment. How insignificant and boring and inconsequential my life seemed now in comparison to all these active, attractive media people. How *small* I felt.

She paused for a moment, so many more years into motherhood than I, and smiled knowingly.

"Well, maybe a small life can be a good life," she said.

I've been doing some pretty strategic "giving up" for the last decade.

The first step came when I quit the security of that full-time magazine office job, a job that I deeply loved, that long defined both me and my social life, that gave me worth and access to the world I was craving. (Or in retrospect, maybe the world I was supposed to be craving.) It was also very obviously a job that was making me unwell with overwork, something I knew and denied. After finally facing the reality that what I was doing—and enduring—was unsustainable, I retreated to full-time freelance writing, which in some ways was like replacing one kind of illness for another.

Given the particular way my generation was taught to approach work (mainly by not caring about much of anything else), I was incapable of rest and existed in terror of scarcity. For me, and my peers, being constantly busy offered a sense of worth, a high-profile punishing job a definition of self. By the time my baseball essay collection came out in the spring of 2017, I realized that the frantic speed at which I had been working for more than a decade—the late nights, the early mornings, the answering work emails on vacation, the acceptance of abuse from superiors and cruelty from social media as part of the job, the terrible work and health habits, the stress and anxiety, the saying yes when I should have said no—was completely unsustainable. Moreover, I was no longer sure this was a life I genuinely wanted, only that it was what I had always done and been applauded for.

Professional writing and publishing is full of the kind of jobs that people respect you for but that don't pay overtime, or even at all well. You may be admired by peers, you may "matter" enough to be part of that beautiful, successful crowd, but you are also constantly on the verge of a health crisis, or an economic crisis, or a total breakdown. (At one office job, I was under so much pressure

I was vomiting regularly, something I bizarrely accepted as part of the deal. I, of course, was lucky to have a job in publishing at all, even if it was literally making me sick.)

That's the thing about our pervasive culture of overwork, regardless of the industry—it's mythmaking. It does everything in its power to make you stay stuck. It builds a mystique around what you do and who that makes you, so much so that you desperately miss the frenzy when it's gone, regardless of how much healthier you have the potential to be in its absence.

I recognized the need to step away from the toxic speed of modern life for a long time before I finally did. It was like I had been circling an idea, trying to get to the bottom of a feeling, but never quite getting there. Fundamental questions always lingered that prevented me from taking the leap: How do you find the balance between doing the work you love and care about, in a way that is sustainable and healthy, while also finding financial stability? Is that even possible? And where does your identity come from if not from work?

It's well and good to say that we should all stop working at this frantic pace, but for many—especially younger workers—that pace is what is necessary not only to stay relevant and in the game but also to survive. The fear that comes with tuning out and turning things down is very real and very justified.

What's worse, an ability to tolerate general mistreatment now seems to be a desired contemporary working trait. Often when I got brave enough to ask where my cheque was, or for a reasonable amount of time to do a job, or to be paid what I was worth, I could almost hear the eyes rolling, my name crossed out on a list of future options. I remember one publisher in particular just went ahead and wished me luck when I asked for a rate similar to what his male columnists were being paid. Another never emailed again after I turned down a single job because of work overload—this after writing for the publication upwards of fifty times. A third stopped getting in touch completely when I said I had a new baby that made the work difficult, as if babies don't eventually grow up. All that reality certainly flies in the face of any "demanding a seat at the table" logic.

I can't entirely credit myself for making the move to embrace a slower pace. Getting pregnant a month after launching my book on baseball was the invitation necessary for a genuine breather. I had the perfect excuse to pare things down, to pull away from my unhealthy addiction to work, and I took it.

After some time spent being forced to slow down, I'm no longer convinced that teetering on the edge of burnout is what success really looks like. I no longer think the only way to matter is by checking your email in the middle of the night or poolside on vacation, by over-scheduling and under-sleeping, by exposing yourself to abuse and destroying yourself in the process of "succeeding." Instead, I'm trying to find ways to resist the delirious pressure to always be producing.

If productivity has become a competitive sport and writing an ongoing rivalry, then I have chosen to bow out of the race.

During the course of my twenty-year career in publishing, I dutifully tried to follow the screed of "knowing your worth," "demanding what you deserve," and "never giving up." Yet so often I ended up in front of a person who informed me there was no way I could have that raise or some time off. I've been told that no, I couldn't have the same leave, or money, or opportunities as my male peers. I've been chastised for wanting to pursue education, for desiring necessary cost-of-living increases, for asking for a better title. I've even been told that simply asking for these things showed a lack of commitment, that I was being "difficult," and that I should feel *lucky* to get what I've been given.

Every time I asked, I knew, without any doubt, that I deserved it. I'd done the research and made the case. I'd known that I was as, if not more, worthy than my (male) peers who were already getting what I was requesting.

While being prodded to follow your dreams and believe that anything is possible seems noble on the surface, the problem lies in the fact that many of us aren't given the community support necessary to sustain that drive. We are consistently told that we can all get a piece of the pie if only we work hard enough, but the pie never gets any bigger, and there are usually just crumbs left on the plate when your turn comes up.

One thing this toxic hustle culture doesn't teach us is just how powerful and healing it can be to simply surrender, give up, and let go. It doesn't tell us how and when to release our grip, or guide us to a place of acceptance where we can be open to what we can become after doing so. It doesn't let on how liberating it can actually be to say no, opt out, and step away.

As much as I long subscribed to the false ethos of possibility that was all around me, as much as I worshipped at the altar of doing my best at all costs, as much as I believed that hard work would always be rewarded, I eventually learned the hard way that I can't actually fly to Florida to cover spring training with third-degree vaginal tearing. I came to understand that I wouldn't be able to make a daily 7 p.m. game start while also being the sole food source for a newborn, and that I really shouldn't record an audiobook in-studio postpartum while wearing an adult diaper. (I mean, I shouldn't have but I did, and while sitting on the tiny awkward stool in the sound booth, I really wished I hadn't.)

In the wake of my daughter's birth, it turned out "anything" is not actually possible, no matter how many times the idea is printed in girl boss books and on pastel-coloured novelty mugs. The well-meaning phrase "we can make this work" may feel like the right thing to say at the time but can often be a lie, and the more people—including other mothers—who perpetuate that deception, the more damaging it becomes.

Sometimes you really just *can't* and you have to give up and walk away. However difficult, however much you feel like a failure as a result, it can often be really healthy and in your best interest to do so.

I think back on my colleague's words at that book launch years ago, and I wonder in the years since my daughter was born if I have actually succeeded in creating a Good, Small Life. I do know, at the very least, I have a better one than I did—one where I have more room to breathe, where I value my own worth over perceived prestige. It took me a long time to get here, and though I haven't been totally successful in finding a way to work within this world I love while still taking good care of myself, I am certainly committed to trying. And not by giving myself a big ol' "anything is possible, girl" speech.

It's a well-worn cliché to say that a baby changes you. Some would even say it is a smug sentiment, spoken by people justifying the fact that their lives have been irrevocably changed. But I don't think it's necessary to have a baby to see the necessity of slowing down—it just happened to be necessary for me. Before I became pregnant with my daughter I was at full sprint every day of the week, neglecting my body, my self-preservation, my true sense of self—and ironically running away from the potential reality of never having her in my life at all. It took time to properly grieve my old identity, but I have since been able to breathe, think, and grow in ways I never would have thought possible.

I've discovered there is great power in the self-compassionate process of consciously letting go and, yes, giving up. Loosening my grip brought uncertainty and disappointment, but it also (eventually) brought me great happiness. In many ways I am starting all over again—I can't go back to being that person who had destructive ambitions, was terrible with boundaries, defined herself by her work, and surrendered her worth to arbitrary assessments.

I'm sure some people will read this and assume I am justifying what has been "lost" or "taken" via the difficult process of becoming a mother, and that's fine. I have certainly had moments when I miss the spontaneity and the autonomy and the accolades I took so deeply for granted, the currently shelved project of seeing every ballpark in the MLB, or the simple luxury of going to the movies alone on a Saturday afternoon. But I also believe there will be people who will read this and recognize their own experience, who will understand there is a beauty in embracing the very things we've been conditioned our whole lives to fight against.

After "giving up" on some of my dreams, I've come to realize that we need to stop telling people we can make things work when we simply can't—or, more accurately, won't actually try to—make them work. We need to stop telling them that they should step up and demand what they deserve, especially if what they really deserve will never actually be available to them. Mothers can't magically twist themselves or their children into spaces that exclude them by design, can't be in multiple places at once, can't do what they need to do and function properly while being resented—or worse, punished—for it.

And I'm more than sure that for every woman who is publicly applauded for strapping her baby to her chest and doing a keynote speech at a conference, there are ten more who just wish they could get the accommodation and support to leave their babies at home.

Maybe when fighting so hard not to give up on your dreams it's important to confirm if they ever really were your dreams in the first place. By what and whose metric was your success even measured?

That night at the library, I stayed in my safe spot at the back of the room until the end of my friend's event, sneaking away stealthily during the eruption of well-earned applause. Not offering any goodbyes, I retreated down the curved steps, through the turnstiles, and out the door into the cool spring night.

I felt a new lightness as I stepped onto the sidewalk, a feeling of freedom that could easily have been attributed to being alone during a time in my life where solitude was incredibly scarce. But as the city night buzzed around me, I knew my mood was tinged with something else entirely. My rumpled shirt and lost gift for small talk no longer mattered at all. The ill fit of my old life that I had felt back in the library meant that something else—something *good*—was possible, if only I could find the willingness to make room.

Giving up, it would seem, could actually be a very good thing.

EPILOGUE

Becoming Better

"And now that you don't have to be perfect, you can be good."

—John Steinbeck, *East of Eden*

Before their children arrived, the women at the local baby story time presumably had busy personal lives and passions and careers and, well, actual *names* beyond "mama." All these powerful, engaging women with varied interests and behaviours and secrets and habits now fighting for a prime spot on a stained primary-colour-blocked play mat at their local library, shooting each other saccharine, passive-aggressive glances while doling out badly received advice about sleep schedules and feeding styles. Withering smiles. Desperate gazes. Each of them just trying to do their best.

The woman to my left talks to her seven-month-old with boundless, (truly) unbelievable energy and bubbly enthusiasm. She is a faucet of adorable cooing kindness that can never be shut off. It exhausts me just to be near her, makes me want to mainline coffee even though I can't because (as I've previously noted so many times that early readers of this book told me I really needed to pare it back) my baby is apparently the world's worst sleeper and I've got to keep my breast milk clean of any hint of caffeine. Exhausted, I irrationally hate the woman to my left, even though a huge part of me wishes I was her, wishes that I could summon that kind of enthusiasm for a librarian with a ukulele.

The mat women say absurd things like "take nice" when the babies tug their toys from each other, a phrase I repeat to my geriatric dog when offering her a piece of my dinner.

"Share, share, share" they chant absently, like an anthem sung so many times that the words lose all meaning.

What happened to them, I would wonder.

Not long after my daughter turned three, I got a message from a friend that a journalist from the paper I used to freelance at regularly was looking for me. The journalist in question needed an "expert" quote for a piece he was writing about baseball and had sent my friend a note, saying he was having a hard time finding my email and could he pass the request along.

His correspondence, forwarded my way, had opened with a particularly cringe-worthy question:

"What happened to her?"

I remember standing in my kitchen, staring at the question on the screen of my phone, and letting out a long, audible sigh. My fears of what *other people* were thinking were finally confirmed.

Nothing, of course, had *happened* to me. I mean, nothing unless you count having a baby, and the subsequent eighteen months of maternity leave that unfortunately closely collided with the onset of the pandemic. Nothing had happened but the unaided struggle of desperately trying to keep a career afloat with little to no childcare. Nothing had happened other than massive budget cuts at the places I once wrote for frequently, or the logistics of a baby making it impossible for me to cover baseball (or baseball not happening at all during COVID).

Nothing had happened to me, unless you count the fact that my worldview had radically shifted, that I was no longer sure I wanted to sacrifice my leisure time, my health, and my sanity for an industry that paid five cents a word for writers to unearth their traumas and then expected them to be grateful for it. Nothing except me starting this book you're reading, only to find it took so many more months to finish than expected—and then even more when the second pandemic wave hit, and more yet with the third.

So often we ask mothers and their struggles to become invisible. We demand that they not take up too much space, not show us the difficult and exhausting realities of their day-to-day, not reveal the struggle to return to "normal." In fact, many professional women are asked to keep their mom selves—their private, vulnerable, and valuable selves—hidden from view in order to maintain any sense of power, professionalism, or success.

Without complaint, mothers must quickly return to somewhere that actually cannot be reclaimed, something long gone—to their "before" body, to their career, to their connections and community, to their former life.

And if you don't get back quickly, and against all odds, there comes that dreaded question:

"What happened to her?"

All that desperate yearning to become a mother, that ache that sat inside me for so long and refused to disappear. I assumed that finally becoming one would actually make me feel more—not less—like myself.

In those very early days, now so long ago they seem like a dream, my daughter wanted only me. Later, as a preschooler, she exerts her burgeoning independence, wants to do everything "by mehself." It's an impulse that shamefully wounds me, that lack of need when I made all of myself so excruciatingly available. But I also realize her confidence is a blessed trait, my increasing uselessness made possible by her security. She has cultivated her precious freedom via the fact that, despite how hard it all was and despite what was lost in the process, I gave myself completely to her.

In the wake of the initial sacrifice of motherhood, the path to postpartum wellness involved a great deal of, yes, rest, but also work—not only on my battered and torn body but also on myself, my values, my overall outlook. Recovery was about patience, self-acceptance, and the kind of self-compassion that was never encouraged and that I had never been good at. True healing necessitated that I—someone who is deeply controlling and hard on herself—be okay with not knowing what was going to happen today, tomorrow, or a year from now. It was about living without that judgment I had long become so good at.

These tough lessons learned in the crash course of "becoming a mom" are lessons that will apply for years to come, the most important probably being that the only way to face monumental change is with a genuine sense of surrender. To weather transition, you have to be soft and pliable, letting go of all your expectations, your schedules, your old life, and your old self. You have to take it as it comes—embrace the challenges of change—because only then can you appreciate it all.

I know now that the more determined I was to be a replica of the person I was before my daughter was born, the more I suffered. Mothering is so culturally underappreciated that in so many ways it forced me to find my own sense of worth. After that final rejection of my old life, my well-being considerably improved—I rested, cooked healthy meals, began to cultivate deep friendships with a smaller number of people rather than surface relationships with many. I took my time and forgave myself for it. And at a certain point, I knew I could never go back to being the person who needed to be in control, who had destructive ambition, who was terrible with boundaries.

Maybe on paper all these changes mean I am not as successful as I once was, and that the question "What happened to her?" (and all that it implies) is not necessarily off-base. But I no longer live in a thick cloud of buzzing anxiety, no longer live in fear of some unknown threat, no longer bury myself under a pile of work in order to avoid the feelings I really need to address.

In *How to Disappear: Notes on Invisibility in a Time of Transparency*, design, culture, and nature writer Akiko Busch writes that "it has become routine to assume the rewards of life are public and that our lives can be measured by how we are seen rather than what we do."

The reality is that the more invisible person I am now is actually the happiest—and certainly the most well—I've ever been. Things are considerably slower than they once were, and I admit there are still moments when I long for the supposed glamour of a more-intense jam-packed literary and journalistic life, when I feel envious of those still out there making noise, even if they have confided in me that it is making them sick too. But looking back, I understand that the more I fought against the current of change—like I had long been taught to do personally and professionally—the more I felt like I was drowning.

Maybe by the old metrics I accomplish little of consumable value, little worthy of discussion. Maybe I'm boring. But after years of panic attacks in bathrooms and a fear of the dark, I can finally breathe. I have the space to live, and grow, and think in ways I never had before. I've forgiven those who needed to be forgiven. I've let go of the things that were harming me. I've made room for opportunities I didn't see as possible.

There is an episode from the second season of *The West Wing*, one I've been thinking about since I saw it more than a decade ago. Titled "Noël," the episode follows White House deputy chief of staff Josh Lyman (played by a young Bradley Whitford), who has been ordered by a superior to consult with a trauma specialist. Throughout the season, Josh has been recovering from life-threatening injuries sustained during an assassination attempt on a colleague, and his PTSD has provoked very public emotional outbursts and panic attacks, largely triggered by innocuous things—like, for example, music.

> "So that's going to be my reaction every time I hear music?" Josh asks in earnest.
>
> "No," the doctor replies.
>
> "Why not?"
>
> "Because . . . we get better."

I am not a presidential aide who has survived a shooting, nor am I triggered by Yo-Yo Ma playing Bach's Cello Suite No. 1, but this simple sentiment resonated so strongly with me that I've carried it with me through recovery and into some pretty major life changes and challenges. No one entrenched in the thick black swamp of their own pain and disarray believes "better" is possible, but it is, in fact, largely inevitable. Without fully realizing when it happened, I am so much better now than I was at being in crowds, at riding the subway, at folding and unfolding a stroller, at being a writer, mother, and human being—all things I genuinely thought I would fail at forever.

This notion of "savouring every moment" of having a baby suggests that it won't get better with time, that good things will only be lost and we should be desperate to hold on to them. But the reality is that things can and do get better as children grow up—because we get better at the job of mothering.

When I was recovering from my trauma, from anxiety disorder, when I was privately tending to my wounds or airing them publicly, I wrote a great deal about how all I wanted to be was okay. I just wanted to work myself up to a level where I could function, live a day without the endless fear and misery rattling around in my head. In retrospect I see what a small request that was. I should have asked for so much more than to just survive. I should have asked to thrive, because now I know that's actually possible.

It isn't advisable to put the pressure of your own self-improvement on your children, but it's impossible for me to deny that the birth of my daughter improved me in countless ways. Her very appearance in the world healed parts of me that were long broken, proved my long-questioned strength, and allowed me to both grow and slow down enough to see a way through what had long been actively destroying me.

Looking at her face in the deepest parts of night stirred the desire in me to move above that waterline, to swim to shore, to thrive.

Now when the question of what happened to me is asked, I know the answer: *I got better*.

The story time mat women offer glaring evidence that, yes, motherhood is pure neurosis. It's a new category of anxiety to add to the pile. But to be honest, as much as motherhood wounds me near constantly with all its tiny arrows of self-doubt, I prefer this kind of worry and self-recrimination to what I endured when I was being treated for PTSD, when I was infertile, when I was overworking myself in an industry that rarely respected me, when I was in endless hours of therapy. I prefer the library story time mat and the women who populate it to being afraid of subways and dark theatres and elevators and impending panic attacks. I prefer the uncomfortable fit of motherhood to being constantly sick and afraid and ashamed, without someone vulnerable and beautiful to protect from harm.

I prefer that as soon as my daughter was born, every pop song on the radio was suddenly about her. That despite so many years of fear, my love for her was unafraid, my devotion was without restraint.

Throughout our lives we all play a lot of roles, some prescribed and some adopted. Some fit better and feel more authentic than others. Some are new and some are old and some are somehow both. Sometimes we hold on tight to the roles that hurt us, just for the sake of holding on to them, not really sure why we're doing it. Sometimes we play roles we're really good at while others completely humble us and make us feel like we've started the work of being a human being all over again. (I can't tell you how many times as a mother I have said out loud "I can't do this" and then realized *I am doing it*.)

As all those silly ukulele-led songs at the library catch in my throat, as my insecurities humble me and I chant "share, share, share" along with the chorus, I know one thing for certain, one thing I may even be embarrassed to admit: I prefer this ridiculous performance to all the others that came before it.

In the long tail of the greatest and hardest gift, I know I want to live open-hearted ways—without fear of judgment, or drive-by derision, or casual cruelty. I want motherhood to lead me to wonder where I once felt worry, to joy where I once experienced cynicism, to relief where I once felt pain. I want to loosen my grip and be earnest, hopeful, and moved by the smallest delights.

Because now I know that "becoming better" is not about forgetting or forgiving, or even moving past harm done. It is about no longer letting the hurt blot out the sun.

ACKNOWLEDGEMENTS

Thank you to the immensely talented Haley Cullingham for treating these tender years with so much generosity and care, and for thoughtfully pushing me further when I needed to be pushed. This book owes so much to your editorial wisdom and guidance, and I am grateful for the time we spent together conversing and carving it out. Further thanks to Eleanor Gasparik, Linda Pruessen, Andrew Roberts, and the incomparable team at McClelland & Stewart and Penguin Random House Canada who made it possible for this book to make its way into the world.

Thank you to Samantha Haywood for being so much more than an agent. I am lucky to walk this long and winding writing and publishing path with you, and am ever grateful not only to have you in my corner but also to call you friend.

Earlier incarnations of passages from *The Lost Season* appeared in *Hazlitt, The London Reader, Prism International, Open Book, Reader's Digest Canada, Broadview Magazine*, and the anthology *Bad Artist*. I'm grateful to the editors who gave me the arena to explore these ideas and the direction to refine them. I'm also grateful to the faculty at the University of King's College Master of Fine Arts in Creative Nonfiction program, and the supportive writing community that grew out of my time there. Thank you to the incredible early childhood educators who provided my daughter with the space to thrive and allowed me the room to write again.

Thank you to those who generously offered grace, kindness, and support during that fragile lost season and beyond: Lindsay Zier-Vogel, Miranda Newman, Jen Sookfong Lee, David P. Leonard, Chi Nguyen, Avril Loreti, Katharine Barnes, Sandra Ghaly Jacqueline Odette, Lucy DeCoutere, Marj Wong, Richard Bloch, and Rose Le Blanc. Thank you to my mom and dad for not only tolerating this bizarre journey I've been on but wholesale supporting it and me without question. Endless love and gratitude to Heather Cromarty for being my daughter's Auntie Panic and my very best friend—I've survived so much because of you and can never say thank you enough.

And to Spencer and Georgia: I am amazed every day that I get to share this beautiful ever-changing life with you both. You are my everything in every season.

NOTES

An earlier version of "Like a Branch from a Tree in a Storm" was published in *Prism International.* An earlier version of "On Not Writing About Motherhood" was published in *The London Reader.* An earlier version of "A Small, Good Life" was published in the anthology *Bad Artist* (TouchWood Editions, 2025). Parts of this work have been adapted from pieces previously appearing in *Hazlitt*, *Open Book*, *Reader's Digest Canada*, and *Broadview Magazine.*

Natalie Wollenberg's puttanesca sauce with roasted eggplant, appearing in "Acts of Nourishment," is from *County Heirlooms: Recipes and Reflections from Prince Edward County* (Assembly Press, 2020).